CW00683693

Namaste,
Geezer

Namaste, Geezer

Life as a fan
and journalist of
Asian heritage

Shekhar Bhatia

FOOTBALL
SHORTS

FOOTBALL SHORTS

Series curator Ian Ridley

First published by Pitch Publishing
and Floodlit Dreams, 2024

Floodlit Dreams

Pitch Publishing
9 Donnington Park,
85 Birdham Road,
Chichester, West Sussex,
PO20 7AJ
www.pitchpublishing.co.uk
info@pitchpublishing.co.uk

© 2024, Shekhar Bhatia

Every effort has been made to trace the copyright.
Any oversight will be rectified in future editions at the
earliest opportunity by the publisher.

All rights reserved. No part of this book may be reproduced,
sold or utilised in any form or transmitted in any form or by
any means, electronic or mechanical, including photocopying,
recording or by any information storage and retrieval system,
without prior permission in writing from the Publisher.

A CIP catalogue record is available for this book
from the British Library.

ISBN ISBN 978 1 80150 978 7

Cover by Steve Leard
Typesetting and origination by Pitch Publishing
Printed and bound in Great Britain by TJ Books Limited

To Milli, my darling daughter
You are my sunshine

Hammer Time

BEING A prepubescent boy of Asian heritage in east London presents plenty of challenges. Add in being a football fan, and a bundle of emotions and experiences increases the series of conflicts. Growing up in the late 1960s and early 1970s – rarity that I was on the terraces of Upton Park – my love for the game, my romance with it, was tainted by fear, hatred and loathing. Back then, young fans expected to encounter vilification from opposing supporters, even maybe to have to run from them. But there were times when I ran from my own West Ham people.

Eventually, my life in football would lead me to occupy a press seat at the World Cup Final of 2022 in Qatar, and arguably the greatest final of them all as Argentina prevailed over France on penalties after a 3-3 draw to see the crowning moment of Lionel Messi's illustrious career. And somehow my enduring love for West Ham would take me to Prague for a triumphant European final in 2023. Long before both, however, my attitudes towards the game and many of its followers were established, even poisoned at times, through some bitter experiences.

Going to football with your father is supposed to be one of life's joyful rites of passage. For me, it was tinged with jeopardy. My dad, Dharam Bir Bhatia, loved the game and wanted me to share that love. He would take me to Upton Park, where we would try and avoid the men selling the National Front's *Bulldog* magazine outside the gates, their eyes bulging with hatred towards us as we passed, their snarls unavoidable.

Such was the hostility in London against people like me and Dad at that time, that we were openly called Pakis and talked down to in mock-Indian accents. 'Gunga Din' and 'curry-munchers' were some of the favoured insults aimed at us. Some people would just utter the word 'Enoch', a reference to Enoch Powell MP, in 1968 the racist deliverer of the rabble-rousing 'Rivers of Blood' speech.

It was strange. These comments and names hurt, but a kind of defence mechanism kicked in. I would avoid these vile characters to try and gravitate towards the safer section of the club's support. After all, I was coming to love West Ham the team, if not all the supporters. There was folklore to them that as a boy I was only hearing about – the 1964 FA Cup win, the 1965 European Cup-Winners' Cup victory, and the Hammers winning the World Cup a year later thanks to Bobby Moore, Martin Peters and Geoff Hurst – none of which I have any memories of as a small child. Yet, several years on from those momentous achievements I had been told about, I felt a hatred towards me that I never understood. No wonder I was a conflicted youth.

Nor did I ever understand why the fans around me, when West Ham played Tottenham, would consistently and collectively hiss for long periods of the match. Only years later did I find out, to my horror, that these disgusting people were celebrating the slaughter of millions of Jews by the Nazis and using the sound to resemble the gassing of the innocents and to taunt rival supporters of a club that has a large Jewish fan base.

I look back now with a mixture of fondness and retrospective fear as I recall my father shouting at Bobby Moore in Punjabi to 'buck up'. If the looks we received from fellow supporters could have killed, we may never have made it back out of the ground. I now see that Dad kept a stiff upper lip in order not to upset his son by revealing his sadness at all this hostility. He was a man – a barrister and a scholar – so much cleverer than his, our, detractors.

When my father deemed me big enough to travel unaccompanied on the 69 or 58 bus to Upton Park, he stopped attending – probably in pain at the animosity we endured each match – and so I would embark on a fortnightly solo ritual. Not that initially I could afford to pay to go in through the turnstiles. Instead, at around 4pm I would board the bus from the hill outside Leyton Underground station and it would drop me a few miles away on Green Street at around 4.25pm. There I would wait until I saw the huge Boleyn gates sweep open outwards and masses of fans leaving minutes before the final whistle. I was like a salmon swimming against the tide as I weaved my way through them to find myself a space on the Chicken Run terracing down one side, or the North Bank or any small space I could squeeze on to. A lot looked at me as if I was some kind of alien, and there were snarls and grunts, but many also looked at me affectionately and with smiles of welcome. I began to feel that people ain't all bad. Inevitably the referee would signal full time within a few minutes of me joining the throng, but getting a glimpse of the men in claret and blue – albeit just for a few seconds – made my week complete. Being young, small and on my own meant that I largely went unnoticed and was therefore left alone by the racist thugs. Some kind souls even lifted me up to sit on the crush barriers so that I had a better view of the game.

All that would change later in my teens when I became more aware and I stood out more. I got a job stacking can after can of baked beans at a Wallis's supermarket on Leyton High Road, which meant that I could occasionally afford to pay at the turnstiles to take in a whole game. The experience was frequently scary – and I became very wary.

It would often start with seeing Asian market traders' stalls being overturned on Green Street, to a soundtrack of 'Sieg Heil' chants, until the police could get there and offer a protective barrier. Then, when I got in the ground and stood on the terraces, I was always on my guard if skinhead 'bovver boys' with their shiny calf-length, steel-toe-capped boots set their sights on me. Kicking in a 'Paki' head was an appealing prospect for them. I would move closer to clusters of people who seemed decent, would constantly think about my escape route, and head for the toilets if they got too close. I missed a fair few goals because of that. I never felt I could just relax and watch the game. I never joined in the singing. I always felt that I was an outsider.

Afterwards, I would get away quickly but could sometimes see that the skinheads had clocked me and were trying to make their way through the crowds of departing fans to get to me. Running from them became second nature. I never did get beaten up. The fear of that happening to me meant I was always one step ahead, too nimble and too clever for them.

Once, I saw a police officer and his dog challenging a skinhead to behave himself. The thug took no notice and answered back loudly, causing the dog to bark at him ferociously. Unabashed, the lout produced a knife from inside one of his boots and began waving the blade, causing the policeman and dog to retreat. This was fifty years ago, long before the knife epidemic that now takes a shocking number of young lives in London.

As much as I was becoming aware of my Asian heritage and origins and it seeming to offend certain sections of the West Ham support, a lot of the racist slurs when I attended games went over my head, I think, or perhaps I was just too preoccupied with Moore, Hurst and Peters to notice more than I did. I did hear words of the 1970s like nig-nog, coon and sambo being shouted around me. And I do remember thinking how strange – and confusing – it was that some people could shout such things then cheer and hero-worship the team's two feted black players of the time, Ade Coker and Clyde Best. Not that Coker and Best were the first. I know that in the late 1960s there was John Charles, who played for England Under-18s and was the first black player to represent the country at any level. Then there was the Cypriot Yilmaz Orhan, who was also of a different racial origin and played a few games.

They all stirred my interest, even in only reading about them later, but Coker and Best were part of that vanguard of players who bravely endured so much abuse from opposing fans. I admired their stoicism. Perhaps it made me think that I should also persevere amid all the adversity and not let others ruin what I loved.

This was the time of the TV character Alf Garnett, the foul-mouthed, racist, misogynist bigot from the sitcom *Till Death Us Do Part*, played by Warren Mitchell. For me, it was a misfortune that Garnett also supported West Ham. While the makers of the programme would insist that their motives were to satirise and ridicule the character and his attitudes, his use of the words Paki and coon would fan the flames of hate against me and other people of colour, giving licence to the imbeciles. I was astonished later in the mid-1970s to see and hear Mitchell unleash some of his Alf Garnett act at half-time at Orient's Brisbane Road on the ground's tannoy system and then tell fans he actually supported Spurs.

It was in this world that it all began, a lifelong relationship with West Ham, a club that would be often dysfunctional and didn't always deserve my love. I withdrew that love after some sorry episodes, but I kept coming back because I grew up in a school of hard knocks where football offered a release and an escape. And in those circumstances, no matter how badly the game can treat you, you can't help but feel a debt of gratitude for how it informed your early life.

West to East

MY FATHER first arrived in Britain from the Punjab in 1956 and would never forget the way the British treated him when he was a student activist against the Raj during the 1930s – beaten by police lathes for supposedly being an agitator. Years later he and his friends would joke that, after the British finally left India and the Viceroy Lord Mountbatten made his nonsense 'At the stroke of the midnight hour' independence speech in 1947, they had decided to follow them and invade Britain to pay back the favour.

Dad returned to the Punjab in 1958 to collect my mother, brother and elder sister. My mother, Ram Chameli Bhatia, could not initially settle in Britain at the west London home my father had rented, however, and her suitcases were placed on top of a wardrobe almost as if she was in a departure lounge and ready to take her family home at a moment's notice.

That all changed when she became pregnant with me and brought me into the world on 9 February 1959 at St Mary Abbots Hospital, Kensington. Years later, working as a journalist covering an election in Tower Hamlets, I would enjoy telling a British National Party member in response to a racist comment he had directed at me that I was born in the Royal Borough of Kensington and Chelsea. It could thus be argued that I was more true-blue British than the morons who wanted me to 'return' to my motherland.

My early years were spent at 166 Blythe Road, Shepherd's Bush and as a pupil of Addison Gardens primary school and – along with my three siblings: brother Bipin Kumar and sisters Chandra Laika and Sarojini – an attendee of Sunday School at the local Methodist Church. We were brought up as Hindus, which basically meant not eating beef, learning to treat people with respect and attending services in various parts of London. We also went to Sikh events in other areas of London. I think Mum and Dad thought Sunday School would have a good effect on us and, as well as the Hindu spiritual book the Bhagavad Gita, we had the Bible in the house. I enjoyed the Sunday School outings to Worthing and, although I would not grow up to be a religious man, I would become a church choirboy a few years later after a big family move across the capital.

That came in 1965, before I had even kicked a football or seen a game. Seeking a bigger house, my parents were so happy to own their first home and my East End roots were sown. I recall us riding in the back of the windowless removal van with our furniture then emerging from the darkness into our Victorian street in Leyton E10, which had survived the Second World War bombing that had devastated much of the area.

I shed tears when my parents gave me a batch of letters written by the ex-school friends and playmates I had left behind in west London for my new life in the east. But in hindsight I could see it was for the best. We now had a three-bedroom house with a garden. And around the corner, in

Station Road, I began to kick a ball against the steps built into one corner of the dead-end street.

I first went to Downsell junior school then Ruckholt Manor secondary near Orient Football Club's Brisbane Road ground. The school had an initiation ritual involving first-dayers being thrown over a wall near the woodwork class and it was an institution where the staff were sanctioned to give you six of the best for any misdemeanour deemed worthy by the 500 or so 11 to 13-year-olds. Thankfully, I never felt the thwack of wood on my posterior, but I do recall a student once grabbed the cane and turned it on the deputy headmaster. As football was my passion, I didn't care much for the cross-country runs and would therefore receive the slipper on my backside from the sports master Mr Davies for (deliberately) forgetting my PE kit.

I began making new friends but there was always venom from others, and some classmates freely used racial terms. Fortunately, I acquired some protection: I made friends with Keith Lindo, who was of Jamaican heritage and the best fighter in the school. He and his brother Clifton remain my friends today. But you pretty soon learn that you do what you need to. Not only did the P-word enter the British psyche, it also became a buzzword used by misguided school friends. In a play on the Shangri-Las' song, 'The Leader of the Pack', one lad, whose parents hailed from the West Indies, would sing 'Shekhar . . . The Leader of the Paks' when he saw me. Bizarrely, he would laugh like a hyena as our white friends chuckled in support.

The relationship between the kids of Afro-Caribbean and Asian heritage was complicated. You might think they would stick together as both knew racial inequality, but although – and it feels strange to say now – we would have 'blacks v whites' football matches in the playground, there was not the solidarity that could have been expected. We couldn't be lumped together. The black community felt more prominent than mine. 'Their' footballers were coming through, and (though still not enough) there were black faces on TV. I didn't know any Asian footballers back then, didn't see them on my screen, and only knew of one TV presenter, a girl called Ayshea Brough, who presented a pop music showed called *Lift Off with Ayshea*. If TV executives did come up with programmes featuring people of colour, they were a painful watch with so-called comedy shows like *Love Thy Neighbour* and *Mind Your Language* that were, to put it mildly, racially insensitive, stereotypical and crass.

Whereas Asians came to Britain individually – save for the 27,000 who arrived in 1972 after being expelled from Uganda by Idi Amin – in many instances Caribbean immigrants arrived together, invited in the post-war Windrush years as jobs needed filling. We came later, less welcome to many in this country. Not that I had any understanding of that at the time. I was just surviving or trying to, a kid in his own world, in his shell and scared of being insulted or beaten up. How can a child not yet aged ten understand what racism is? It was difficult to deal with and hard to know why the hate existed.

Teachers did their best to interest me in woodwork, metalwork, religious education and maths, though my main interest was in English. I was not a studious pupil, however, and I found myself in my final year, aged 13, planted in a bottom set. This was the group of perceived educational also-rans: kids thought to be uninterested, without ambition and destined for dead-end jobs (if they could even get a job). Such was the lack of establishment care for those kids who had fallen into class 3C, teachers would sometimes fail to turn up to stand in front of the blackboard. Instead, playful mayhem would ensue. Desks would be overturned, cartoon characters drawn on the blackboard and seven-inch vinyl singles (mostly reggae) spun on a record player brought in by a pupil who actually went on to become a successful party DJ. There was also the odd scrap and I saw kids beaten up for next to nothing – including me, twice by black lads who left me with a black eye and were made to apologise to my father. I noted how it was done and twice did it to others when crossed – just a quick punch to the mush. You did what you needed to do, though to my shame, I also whacked one kid for no reason and left him in tears.

I never stopped to wonder how I fell into the bottom class, but in my mind the kids in 3C were not losers or any less important than those in class 3A. Maybe it was because I was a shy, softly spoken, gangly and largely uncommunicative lad and that, as instructed by my parents, I always wore my school blazer and on occasions carried a briefcase, just like the geeky Will in the TV series of much later, *The Inbetweeners*. Somebody once told me that I was gullible. I asked them what gullible meant. I appeared to others as someone with not very much to say, though I did once ask a teacher what the point in living was.

There was a glint of hope for my class when we won a school contest to bring food in for the Harvest Festival. A case of oranges from the son of a grocer – one point per piece – put us in pole position and we were rewarded with a day trip to Southend-on-Sea. There we kicked a ball about on the stony beach and I first felt the softness of a girl's lips – in the romantic setting of a toilet cubicle in the Kursaal amusement park. On the coach trip home I felt all kinds of worry particularly as (despite her consensual puckering-up) she might tell my parents.

My fortunes were to change for the better later in that year when I wrote an essay on how 'Mother Nature has lost her job' (the title is all I remember about it), which saw me propelled into class 3A. On my first Monday morning with my new classmates, several moved to other desks as I tried to take a seat next to them.

In my solitude and awkwardness, I remained alive with only one intention: to play for West Ham United. I would hold up pictures of Bobby Moore in his claret and blue shirt and marvel at the way the colours changed to a different, beautiful hue in different light. I took part in trials and practice matches for the school football team and I had some skills, scored the odd goal. On one occasion our side were awarded a penalty. Most of the lads wanted to take the kick and pleaded with the teacher to be allowed to. Being a shy boy who felt he had to suppress his passion for football because he didn't want to upset other, stronger kids, I did not put my hand up. But the teacher, feeling sorry for the outsider, chose me. I duly dispatched the spot kick and the gratifying back-slapping and feeling of acceptance has probably never really been matched since.

Sadly, I was never good enough for the first team, however, and I became a fixture in the second team. I would look on in envy as the lads chosen to represent the first team were picked out and told to report to the playground on Saturday mornings to catch the bus to school stardom, and I would listen enviously to their footballing heroics when school resumed on Monday morning. I guess I wasn't cocky or aggressive enough, either. Long before Ridgeway Rovers became David Beckham's club, I tried out there but just fell by the wayside.

Still, my passion for the game did not diminish, fuelled by *Match of the Day* on our black and white TV and a somewhat relentless search for stickers of footballing heroes for my 'Soccer Stars in Action: First Division' book. The sticker collection became priceless to me when my father turned up to the opening of a sports shop in Leytonstone High Road by Geoff Hurst – the event cruelly held on a school day – to ask him to sign my album. I would run my fingers over the signature in reverence, my awe-struck eyes just like Mowgli's when he meets the snake Kaa in the Disney film *The Jungle Book*. To this day I cherish the book, with its handwriting of the man who scored a hat-trick for England in a World Cup Final. It is symbolic to me in so many ways. Back then, it was my bible and remained at my bedside. Each night I would examine the statistics and pictures and simply dream that I belonged in – might even become a part of – that world.

On one page was Allan Clarke of Leeds United, on another Kevin Hector of Derby County, both great strikers of the day. A flip of a page, each bearing 15 faces, would bring me to George Best of Manchester United and Mike Summerbee of Manchester City. Years later I would get the chance to tell Mr Summerbee, when I bumped into him as he visited a client in London as a bespoke shirt designer, how I would almost drool over these sticker photographs, that I bought for 3d a packet from the local newsagent. (I was also guilty of theft on one occasion when I nicked a packet while the shopkeeper had her back turned. However, when she swivelled and faced me again I saw the look on her face and I knew she knew. The fact that she said nothing and let me walk out with my stolen loot still pains me today.)

Football – both playing, if only for the seconds, and watching – developed from a passion into an obsession. I could regularly be seen kicking a ball around the steps close to Leyton underground station. I recall my parents again being deeply upset when a friend of theirs told them he would witness me and my ball occupying the pavement each night as he returned from a day at the office. 'This boy will never do anything in his life. He will waste his time kicking that damn football around instead of focusing on his studies,' he informed them, to their dismay.

When summer came, I headed down to Leyton Cricket Ground to watch Essex play and cheered on Asif Iqbal of Kent and the late Bishan Bedi of Northamptonshire. I was also thrilled to witness Eddy Merckx whizzing along on his bike in a race on Hackney Marshes, close to where I ventured out to watch speedway races too.

My father, worried about my lack of interest in studying, decided that I would not join my classmates in transferring to Tom Hood Senior High School, which was also the alma mater of my hero Bobby Moore. Dad was unhappy that I seemingly wanted to focus more on sport and riding my bike than attaining the highest marks at school. He had trained as a barrister in the High Court in Lahore when it was still in India and part of the Punjab, and would often tell me he had hopes that I would study law too, become a judge in the High Court of London and that I'd sign my warrants with a gold-nibbed pen that he would buy me.

Maybe he was hoping I would fulfil his dream. He knew when he came to England that his legal qualifications would not be valid and so he worked initially as a sales rep for a sports equipment company based in India called Pioneer in New Delhi's Connaught Square. I recall him telling me how he travelled to Blackpool to meet the great Stan Mortensen, who had a sports shop in the town. After Dad returned to England from India in 1958, he became a carpet salesman.

And so in 1972, instead of Tom Hood School, I was sent to one that was supposedly better, McEntee Senior High in Walthamstow, a four-mile bus ride away from Leyton. It had also been the school my brother, nine years older than me, had attended and for that reason the school accepted me. My first day was petrifying. The boys looked much older, much rougher and much bigger than me. And apart from a handful of other transfers from Ruckholt, I knew nobody. I was plunged further into my solitude by the lack of familiar faces, and the violence around me scared me to my core.

A ginger-haired greaser with a crucifix earring smashed a teacher in the face. Another two teenagers brawled until both lads were black and blue. One portly bruiser smacked a lad so hard that his head cracked against the gym floor while the teacher looked on and said nothing. Others showed off flick-knives and openly smoked drugs. At the gates you could buy knocked-off shoes from Ravel, stolen cigarettes or seven-inch pop singles that were manufactured at a local factory. After school and at Boy Scouts at Ivy Farm on Tuesday evenings, I was routinely bullied and beaten up by groups of boys, although I never told my parents, not wanting to upset them. It wasn't just physical pain I felt. I felt ashamed, though I had done nothing wrong.

But McEntee had another, more appealing, side for a kid who loved sport: it had a swimming pool and lawn tennis courts – hence it being seen as supposedly a 'better' school in many ways – and football pitches. Perhaps here, my dreams of developing as a player and donning the claret and blue, lifting the FA Cup and being chaired aloft by my team-mates at Wembley would come to fruition. After all, everyone at the school talked about Brendon Batson, who had once studied at the school and played on these pitches before going to form, with Laurie Cunningham and Cyrille Regis, West Bromwich Albion's 'Three Degrees' (a term I would come to detest when I understood more about the game's culture). Sadly for me, it again became clear that I was not going to be good enough, and the second team would be the summit of my achievements. My prospects of being called up to the first team nosedived when, during one second XI game when playing at centre-half in heavy rain and mud, I ducked as a corner came in, leaving an opposing forward to head home. I heard my team-mates grumbling as we made our way back to the halfway line about how they thought I was going to head the ball clear. 'Do you know how heavy that thing is with all the rain and mud?' I moaned back. I think I knew then that I didn't have what it took.

The bar was high at my school, mind. In the first team were players like Steve Neville, who would go on to play for Exeter and Southampton, and my classmate Terry Hurlock, who became a Millwall and Glasgow Rangers legend and hardman. Terry was also the best fighter at school. Fortuitously, we became friends – and remain so to this day. I would watch in awe from the sidelines as Tel and Co. took teams apart. It wasn't unusual for him to bang in five or six goals a match. We all knew he was destined for greatness.

Instead, I concentrated more on watching the game. And gradually that gave me the idea of what I wanted to be.

The Mysterious Orient

WEST HAM were my first love and will always be my foremost love. But there was another club local to me who came to attract my attention and affection from a young age, even if at first I paid scant notice on my journey to school to what Leyton Orient's high-walled Brisbane Road ground actually was.

My first recollection of the noise that emerged from over the walls and into the red ash field where I would also kick my Mexico '70 black and white-panelled ball came one Saturday afternoon when I was 11 years old. I believed it was a men's choir that must have been singing. I had never heard anything like it. I also imagined there must be some dancing going on in the arena and that people were clapping and singing along with the entertainer. I had an image of a Cossack performer squatting and leaping from his haunches and waving his arms. Or perhaps a ballerina pirouetting in front of thousands of men with deep voices and clapping along. A child's imagination… What could be going on in there? The walls were too high for me to climb so that I might see.

I discovered what all the partying was about a few weeks later when I made an unlawful entry into the ground – and in a painful and undignified manner. A group of lads gave me some help up by joining hands so that I could leap on to them and bounce over the wall. Except that the drop on the other side was around 10 feet. My fellow invaders, some of whom were taller and didn't need a lift up, became angry with me as I sat on the top of the wall, blocking the way but fearing the drop. They could hear the snarling stewards heading our way to apprehend us and so somebody pushed me off the wall. I landed seeing stars, as the others climbed over my aching body then scurried into the grassy banks and disappeared into the stands. Meanwhile, I was grabbed by my grey school V-neck jumper, though pity thankfully kicked in among the stewards and they allowed the crying kid to go free and experience his first entry into a football match.

The magic hit me straight away: an ocean of humanity; a sea of love – or so it felt to one so young and unfamiliar with how a crowd could turn – for the men on the pitch. I was hooked immediately, despite worries that I might go deaf after a home Orient fan rattled his wooden clacker for the entire match just inches from my ears. I was absorbed by the sight of the red home shirts, the quagmire of the pitch with the mud flying through the air and the whole theatrical experience. For the life of me, I cannot recall who Orient were playing that day or the names of the home players, though they were soon to become familiar. The first character who made an impression on me was the trainer Peter Angell, who would run on to treat the injured stars with a football cut in half full of water and a sponge. He always seemed to have a grin on his face.

There was a bald-headed centre-half called Terry Mancini. I felt for him when he headed the heavy leather ball and an elderly cockney gentleman next to me, in a phrase that could have come from a speech bubble in a cartoon in one of the papers, said: 'Crikey, 'is 'ead ain't 'alf gonna 'urt in the morning.' The goalkeeper Ray Goddard was catlike as he sprang through the air and always followed his goal kicks with admiring glances checking their trajectory right until the ball landed.

Then there was Barrie Fairbrother, the forward whose straggly hair and beard gave him the look of a Beatle. He scored the winning goal in the 1971 FA Cup fifth-round encounter against Chelsea in extra time and the *Match of the Day* cameras were there to capture the moment – as well as me in the crowd. I positioned myself on the wall along the halfway line and sat on it with my legs clearly visible. I wanted the BBC to know where I was and for millions of others to see me on their televisions. That night I ran my finger along the blurred image of my torso as *Match of the Day* relayed the highlights in black and white and the cameras, following the action, panned at speed past me. My parents were bemused at my excitement as I pointed my finger at the screen shouting, 'There I am. That's me.'

There were many memorable days at Brisbane Road, none more so than when Leicester City were the opposition, Jimmy Bloomfield their manager, some time in the early 1970s. I hadn't been able to find a wall to climb over that day and was unable to sneak in behind any supporter going through the turnstiles, and so I had to wait until the last 15 minutes or so when the gates opened to get in. I took up a position among the paying supporters on the southern terrace behind Leicester's goal.

My parents had given me a giant orange to eat and it was beginning to annoy me stuck in my pocket. I peeled it and, completely out of character, began chucking the orange peel at the City goalkeeper, Peter Shilton. One slice landed in front of him as he prepared to take a goal kick. Another could be seen nestled around the penalty spot as I increased the strength of my throws. Shilton looked in my direction for a second but could not establish who the phantom orange-peel chucker was. However, all this was not lost on the local constabulary and, with the game stopped as police moved into action, I felt the heavy hand of Her Majesty's force on my lapel. I also felt every pair of eyes among the thousands in that stadium trained on me in my moment of shame at having stopped the match. The officer began escorting me towards the exit as other supporters returned to the action and no longer paid me any attention at all. But the final whistle blew just as I was being ejected from the ground and the bored police officer went to cuff me behind the ear, missing by inches and then shooing me off, warning me I would be in greater trouble if there was a next time.

Soon, Orient became a way of life, being much easier to get to from my home near Leyton underground station and bunk into than my real love, West Ham. I first heard the voice of Frank Sinatra over the tannoy as the DJ/announcer played his songs almost on loop. I recall, too, 'Tijuana Taxi' by Herb Alpert, which is still the tune the team run out to, though from dressing rooms and the tunnel now on the opposite side of the ground.

I was, I suppose, an annoying little kid and on one quiet day of the school holidays, I crept into Brisbane Road with my new black and orange plastic football. With nobody seemingly around, I ran on to the pitch and booted my ball towards the net and prepared to throw my arms up in glory to the empty stands. I missed and my ball crashed against the advertising hoardings. A few minutes later the unhappy groundsman appeared and chased me off the pitch and threw me out. I fibbed that Orient's Indian-born star Ricky Heppolette was my big brother, but my pleas fell on deaf ears.

Getting a job selling programmes for a while at the gates of Brisbane Road allowed me to get in free too. Once, I saved myself a beating when cornered and confronted by Queens Park Rangers thugs who asked me which team I supported by telling them I was from Shepherd's Bush and that it was QPR. They didn't believe me, of course, and asked me which road I lived in. When I told them Blythe Road, a popular and well-known thoroughfare, they were dumbfounded and let me pass.

I was fascinated by the TV commentators and their cameramen and would spend much of games staring in wonderment at the gantry high above the pitch. Health and safety concerns were less rigorous in those days, and top commentators like Hugh Johns and Brian Moore would scramble unsteadily up and down an angled wooden ladder to get to and from their commentary positions. I would wait, long after the final whistle, for them to emerge and once asked Mr Johns if he knew the Nottingham Forest score. I knew he worked for the Midlands company ATV and when he said, 'Well, I know they were one down at half time,' my heart glowed. He had said words that he might say on the TV, but his words had been for me exclusively and not for his audience of millions. Brian Moore once let me carry the silver canisters containing film reels across the pitch after London Weekend Television had recorded Orient beating Sunderland 1-0 with a Terry Parmenter goal.

As well as the TV commentators, I became interested in the reporters who covered football. Before school each morning, I would read my father's newspaper, the *Daily Telegraph* and its football writers, Robert Oxby and Donald Saunders, became my conduits to the action through their words. I was captivated by how they described key moments of matches that had taken place only the night before. The drama contained in each report would play on and on in my mind. I wanted to be like them, going from ground to ground, sitting in the best seats, watching the greatest games and seeing my name in print above stories too.

Orient and the *Daily Telegraph*'s wonderful sportswriters were conspiring in sending me towards a life on the road and the opportunity to meet my sporting idols. And I showed that I was priming my skills for a life in journalism while walking home from Ruckholt and taking a diversion to gawp at Brisbane Road once more.

The *Evening News,* the now-defunct London evening paper, had reported that Manchester City star Ian Bowyer was in talks to sign for Orient. I was loitering around the ground with no serious intent after school when I saw a shiny grey Jaguar parked outside. Closer inspection of the tax disc – in those days each windscreen had to have one – showed that the vehicle tax had been paid in Manchester. I dashed home, and using my father's green desk phone, I telephoned the *Evening News.* The switchboard put me through to the sports desk, whose representative I informed that Mr Bowyer had been at Brisbane Road. They would pass it on, they said. I have no idea whether they used it. The next day, I also duly reported to my schoolmates that Bowyer would be playing for Orient. Despite their incredulity, my first scoop was proven a few days later when it was confirmed he had signed along the dotted line and become an Orient player. He marked his arrival with a hat-trick in his first match.

George Petchey was then the manager and the kid who had believed there was a sea of love for the players and manager at his first game had grown to shudder as the abuse rained down from the stands whenever Orient were wretched. These were grown men ranting and raving – and with such venom! – at someone who appeared to me to be just a little old bald bloke seated in a claustrophobic concrete dugout. I felt for Petchey, not realising that was the way football operated (which is to say, you sing when you're winning, but angrily swear like a trooper when things are not going that well).

Petchey, however, took the O's to the edge of glory in May 1974 when his team needed a victory over Aston Villa at home to secure promotion to Division One, a feat only achieved once before, when they went up with Liverpool in 1962. Due to my Saturday job in Wallis's supermarket, by now I could afford to fork out the cost of a ticket and this was the match of matches; Orient were to join the likes of Liverpool (who had stayed in the top flight in 1962 and become huge, while Orient had gone straight back down), Chelsea, Arsenal and Leeds United in the top tier. I could see the celebrations had begun early as I skipped through Coronation Gardens, adjacent to the ground. Several Orient fans lay outstretched on the grass having clearly downed a few too many beers in the hours before kick-off.

Brisbane Road was buzzing like never before and I was crammed in behind the goal on the southern end of the stadium, on tiptoes. Villa had nothing to play for but they played out of their skins. I recall Ray Graydon taking a penalty as I watched like a meerkat, my head popping up and down along with the others on the terrace, hoping that somehow he would sky the ball towards Coronation Gardens. He didn't, and Villa went 1-0 up. Mickey Bullock equalised later with a header, but Orient just could not score the winning goal that would have taken them back to the top flight. I remember the *Daily Mirror* describing the Villa defence the next day as 'Scrooges'.

By now I had accepted that I wasn't going to be good enough to play the game professionally and was leaning towards wanting to be a football writer. It was meeting two great footballers that confirmed it for me. If I couldn't play alongside these heroes, then I could at least still walk among them. The first was Sir Trevor Brooking, who happily gave me his autograph outside West Ham (while Clyde Best did a runner to escape the schoolboy scrum that had engulfed him). The second was John Toshack, who had just played for Cardiff City at Orient. At the end of the game on my way out, I somehow found myself in the Brisbane Road VIP reception area. As I made my exit to the street, I saw a huddle of men. They were chatting to the footballers. Who were they, I wondered? I quickly learned that these gentlemen were 'reporters'. Like Messrs Oxby and Saunders. And I quickly discovered that they got in free, got to talk to the players and got paid for it too. This was a turning-point moment for me. *I want to do that*, I thought as I sauntered down Leyton High Road towards home.

I had no idea who this daunting and dominating guy who had just signed my autograph book was either. Just some geezer talking to the chaps in the raincoats who had stopped his briefing to appease the schoolboy intruder. And then I noticed alongside his squiggly signature he had written 'J. Toshack' in plain capitals. This gentleman, who went on to be a Liverpool and Wales great, and Real Madrid manager, had clearly been touched by a doe-eyed kid requesting an autograph, seen that he had no idea who he was asking and then taken the book back and written his name out in capitals. And all between chatting to the men in rain macs. Even at such a tender age, I could see what humility and kindness were about – perhaps highlighted in contrast to the vitriol and nastiness I received from certain quarters at school – and the mantra of my McEntee headmaster Mr Grey came into my head: 'Manners maketh the man.' I would never forget John Toshack's charming, thoughtful moment – nor the brigade of men in macs.

I liked being among my heroes and now I had seen a pathway to making it happen.

The Rag Trade

WHILE FOOTBALL felt like it could open up the world for me, the staff at McEntee School, particularly the careers officer, seemed set on closing it down.

I was halfway through my A Levels at the age of 17 when I was sent to see the careers officer. The bespectacled gentleman with the Einstein hairstyle asked me what occupation I had set my eyes on. Perhaps he was bored with pupil after pupil telling him they wanted to be astronauts, film stars or airline pilots and was used to telling them that they needed to be more realistic. Or perhaps there was a more sinister element. Because when I told him that I would like to be a journalist and that sport really interested me, back came the answer:

'You will never be a journalist. Your sort of people work in accounting or banks.' *Your sort?* Was it that I was from Leyton, or did he mean something else? Either way, I felt like telling him to fuck off but I feared being expelled and having to face my father's wrath. He gave me a piece of paper with his recommendations outlining what options I had as I left bewildered and confused.

Soon, I found myself in an interview at NatWest, who had clearly been prevailed upon to check me out to see if I was suitable for a life in banking. I was so perturbed that I could end up stamping cheques or selling fixed bonds, that when the interviewer quizzed me on what I wanted out of a career with his bank, I decided on drastic action and placed my feet on his glass desk. That had the desired effect and I was quickly shown the door.

Being told that journalism was not for me only made me more determined and I became besotted by the profession. I began to read every newspaper in the library at Leyton Town Hall and hero-worshipped reporters and envied them their bylines. My imagination ran loose as I dreamed of filing stories from the biggest arenas from the biggest sporting occasions. And, like many a reporter of my generation, I loved the film *All the President's Men,* with Dustin Hoffman and Robert Redford as Carl Bernstein and Bob Woodward, the two *Washington Post* reporters who broke the story of the Watergate and Richard Nixon scandal.

I wrote to every national newspaper, spelling mistakes and all, telling the editors that I was their future star correspondent. None of them seemed to agree. Instead, it was the *Waltham Forest Guardian* who took pity on me. Not only did they write back but they also asked me to come into their offices opposite the art-deco Walthamstow Town Hall for a chat. I skipped along on cloud nine for days before the time came for the interview. This time there was no chance at all of my size 11s being placed on the editor's desk.

The editor Rex Pardoe, whose passion for newspapers would lead him to say that journalists shouldn't get paid for a job they loved doing, was as friendly as he was mysterious. He was a smart, gangly, greying Tottenham Hotspur-supporting man who somehow had the art of making you feel relaxed but at the same time keeping you on your toes with his sharp, intellectual wit. I was too young, maybe too stupid and certainly not worldly enough to chat on an equal level with this gentleman who interrupted our interview discussion several times to grab sheets of papers and rush in and out of the newsroom. (I later discovered that these were page proofs that had been edited and typeset before being put on the huge hot metal presses at the back of the building to be turned into full newspapers by the printers.) Afterwards, as I stepped out into that heatwave summer of 1976 with my blue Adidas bag over my shoulder and headed back to school, I didn't really have a clue whether I had made a good impression, but a few weeks later a letter dropped on to the doormat of the family home: I had a job.

After the supermarket shelf-stacking and aisle-sweeping that I was determined would not be my future, my 'proper' working life had begun. I immediately loved the freedom to roam that came with being a self-proclaimed star reporter for what seemed to be known by everyone as 'the local rag'. The *Waltham Forest Guardian* was, though, an excellent paper from the days when they were well staffed and read by all as a big part of the community.

It produced some of the finest writers and reporters for Fleet Street, including the *Daily Mail*'s celebrated sportswriter Jeff Powell MBE, the former head of *Channel Four News* Dorothy Byrne and *The Mirror*'s veteran war correspondent Anton Antonowicz.

Also seated in the newsroom beside me was David Grant, who went on to have a string of top-ten hits and appeared regularly on *Top of the Pops* with his band, Linx. Their songs included the dancefloor classic 'You're Lying' and he even had the Chic guitar genius Nile Rodgers record with him on his hit album *Intuition*. I was there one night in the Euston recording studio to hear it being put together. David never quite 'felt' newspapers as I did, though, and I didn't really expect him to hang around with us long. Across his typewriter, he had the message: 'All the world is a stage. . . David is the star.' He now also presents TV programmes and has a Saturday breakfast show with his wife, Carrie Grant, on BBC Radio London.

While golden weddings, summer fetes and reporting on Leyton Wingate in the Isthmian League at their Lea Bridge Road Stadium were never going to be enough for a talented singer, for me they became a way of life. And when Anton Antonowicz took me under his wing, my skills developed quickly. He was a cool dude with a swagger and I liked his way of getting stories told in the first paragraph and his use of alliteration to make his writing almost poetry-like. Dorothy Byrne, seven years older than me and who provoked a schoolboyish crush in me, also mentored me and helped fuel my hunger for stories. She was university educated, unlike me, and wore a beret that gave her a strong air of left-wing politics. She certainly had forthright views. In addition to her award-winning documentaries and journalism, Dorothy went on to become a leading academic and president of Murray Edwards College, Cambridge University, and remains one of my closest friends.

The two were active in a strong National Union of Journalists branch, but I just wanted to have fun and skip around the borough, notebook and pen in hand. I did join the union after chatting with my father, ever a Labour voter, and taking his advice. It brought me closer too to the rest of the journalists and this was to prove invaluable during the brutally frozen 'winter of discontent', which kicked in between November 1978 and February 1979. At first, I wanted nothing to do with it, having become used to my weekly pay packet and concerned at it being withheld, but a quick call by Ms Byrne to my father ensured that I took my 2am turn getting out of bed to picket our printing plant.

During that strike some of my colleagues were arrested for little more than having loud voices when picketing it seemed to me, but I escaped. For a while at least. After the strike, my turn to be handcuffed came for simply trying to do my job (primarily because I wanted to see my words and my name in print). I remain convinced that racism had a lot to do with it as well.

It was the autumn of 1979 and just a usual evening, with me playing Space Invaders in the Coach and Horses pub in Leyton High Road, near the Orient ground. As I took my last sip from my fizzy drink and departed, the place went mad with police rushing in and cop cars surrounding the venue, blue lights flashing and sirens wailing. I dashed to my Ford Cortina to retrieve my small Olympus camera and hurried back to start snapping away at the mayhem that ensued.

I had no idea what was behind the raid but police were dragging people from the pub and scuffles were breaking out. I turned my lens on a guy struggling to break away from a man in a suit who would turn out to be a plain-clothes detective from the Metropolitan Police. The suit turned on me, knocked my camera to the ground and kneed me in the balls before arresting me. My camera was returned to me on the bus to which they took me, but the film had been ripped out. I spent most of the night in a cell at Leyton police station and some months later appeared before Waltham Forest Magistrates, charged with obstructing a police officer in the execution of his duty. I spent some of those hours in the clink thinking it might be safer to stick to football reporting. The case became something of a *cause célèbre*, with journalist supporters protesting outside, TV coverage and my name featuring in newsprint. It was not the way I wanted my name to be seen by readers.

After a hearing lasting several hours, I was cleared. The court saw through the detective's claims that I had got in his way while he was arresting a violent prisoner and that the flash of my camera had blurred his eyesight, forcing him to arrest me. The NUJ barrister asked him what happened to the 'violent prisoner' and he had no answer. Meanwhile another copper, whom I had never seen before, gave evidence that he had asked me to stand on a street corner to take my pictures and I had refused. I noticed the eyebrows of one of the three magistrates raise towards the ceiling during the police evidence.

I walked free and recall thinking about all those similar young men who had appeared in the same court where I had covered their cases and heard them claim they were being framed. I successfully sued the Met for wrongful arrest, won a small compensation and gave some back to the NUJ. Later I withdrew my complaint against the officer after his superior visited me and my father at home. The superior was pleading, saying the officer's promotion had been held up and that he had a wife and young children to support.

During my subsequent journalistic career, I would come to believe that Britain has the best police force in the world, having seen cops in action elsewhere, but this was a shameful example of what was going wrong during the late 1970s and early 1980s against innocent Londoners, most frequently against people of colour but also those who dared question or get in the way of the police and their often law-unto-themselves tactics.

I took comfort in football and badgered the sports desk to let me cover local non-league games. Leytonstone and Ilford's Granleigh Road ground, along with Walthamstow Avenue, became regular haunts. It was at the former that I caught up again with my old schoolmate Terry Hurlock. He almost broke the net with a 30-yard stunner on a cold night, which I duly reported. Soon, Terry would be signing for Brentford. I recall the Leytonstone boss John Still, who would later manage Dagenham & Redbridge and Luton Town in the Football League, being so polite and patient as this puppyish reporter tried to muster a few intelligent questions and conceal his excitement.

I left the *Waltham Forest Guardian* and joined the *Newham Recorder* in late 1979, perhaps thinking that because their offices were closer to Upton Park, I might get near my West Ham heroes, maybe get to cover some games. The reality was that, after the greenery of Waltham Forest, the harsh, cold concrete and tower blocks of Newham were an eye-opener. Sometimes, the stories the paper covered might have led the readers to believe they were living in a gun-riddled corner of New York. In one of my early weeks there, there was a senseless murder by two brothers and their father after a pub dispute. Their victim's body was found the next morning on Wanstead Flats, which my father had named 'Leyton Airport' when he used to take me there as a boy to watch locals flying model aeroplanes. I was sent to cover the committal at Stratford Magistrates' Court and saw the three accused hunched together in the dock, looking bemused but also as if they were enjoying the attention. It occurred to me that they were from such an impoverished and neglected background, that the focus on them was a welcome change to living life ignored by society and at the bottom of the social strata.

It pretty soon became clear to me that the paper already had an excellent sports desk, enriched by the contributions of the legendary West Ham photographer Steve Bacon, and it looked like it was going to be a long time before I would be gaining any access to the promised land of the press box at West Ham. And so, after being on the paper for just ten tough weeks, I decided I needed a holiday, taking myself off to India for the first time. I loved the country so much that I ended up staying for almost five months. Not surprisingly, I returned to find that my job had gone.

But the *Tottenham Weekly Herald* was hiring and with it came the opportunity to report on Glenn Hoddle and his Spurs at White Hart Lane, just down the road from the newspaper's offices. We West Ham fans called them the Spuds, but I wasn't going to let my prejudices get in the way. It was not uncommon to see the likes of Steve Archibald, Ossie Ardiles or Mark Falco strolling down Tottenham High Road. Chris Hughton once scraped the snow off his car for me and photographer Tony Wedderburn and laughed as he said: 'The things I have to do for a photograph!'

It was another newsy area, and the price to be paid for my press seat at White Hart Lane was also covering stories such as stabbings and drug arrests. There was one chilling episode lasting several months when a sexual predator who became known as 'The Tottenham Rapist' stalked the streets of north London. We were as keen to catch him as the police were and around the newsroom we had various headlines and posters of police photofits of what they believed he looked like. The shocking truth hit us hard when it was revealed that the man police would catch, charge and eventually jail was the boyfriend of one of the office staff. He had become a familiar face in the building when he would pick her up from work and would often stop to look at the wanted and appeal posters for crimes he had committed.

The *Weekly Herald* folded in 1982 and I received a £3,000 redundancy cheque. I splashed out on a new VW Golf and started pestering Fleet Street for work.

Football/News

MY GROUNDING on local papers had felt like a long time, or so the impatience of youth told me. But very quickly after being made redundant, I got the work I wanted. Or thought I wanted.

I became a freelance football reporter with the *Mail on Sunday* and was dispatched to cover such teams as Notts County, Grimsby and Leicester City in the old Football League lower divisions. I soon discovered, however, that although I was watching football, all the new pressures to meet demanding deadlines took much of the joy away. For a match like Fulham v Newcastle, it was 500 words for the northern edition on the final whistle followed by the 'nanny goats' (quotes) from the manager. Then, less than an hour later, it was a similar word total for the southern edition and what their manager had to say. At best I found it hard going, at worst I struggled to cope.

There was no internet or laptops, just typewriters, or pen and paper, and desk phones from which to file your report. Martin Samuel – then of Hayters sports agency and who would go on to be one of the very best of sportswriters for a host of papers including the *Daily Mail* and *The Times* – would kindly ensure my phone was set up and working and would always offer me a smile and a warm greeting.

I managed to make it through two seasons before being found out when I was sent to Highbury for an Arsenal game and I sat nervously among some of Britain's leading football-writing operators, watching in shy admiration as they filed their meticulous and sometimes poetic pieces while I laboured for an intro and wondered why I was putting myself through all this. Imposter syndrome played a nervy part in my psyche, for the press box was an unforgiving place. There were very rare welcomes from the football writers (who I later discovered my news colleagues contemptuously labelled 'groin strains' because of the dull injury stories they would file). Sometimes I would have to clamber over stretched legs to reach my seat, apologising along the way. I did not feel like one of them, and I wasn't one of them. I believed some deliberately blocked my path – physically and metaphorically. And if I wanted to ask a question of a manager among a huddle, I was elbowed out of the way and found it hard to hear what was going on.

The worst example of how I could be treated in the company of 'mainstream' football writers came much later, at the 2019 Women's World Cup semi-final between England and the USA in Lyon. I was working for *Mail Online* and I'd been diverted from a news story in Paris to cover the match, particularly the supporters who provided a very different vibe to the one I had experienced at England men's matches. I picked up a last-minute accreditation and when I walked into the media room, I felt sure I was met with looks of dismay by some of the sports reporters. It's not uncommon for news journalists to be regarded with some suspicion as they are on a different beat.

As the England manager Phil Neville gathered with a huddle of journalists following his team, I placed my iPhone under his nose to record the briefing. My simple attempt at doing my job was ended by a sports hack from *The Sun* newspaper, who snatched my phone, ended the recording and held on to the device until Mr Neville had finished his briefing. The phone was returned to me and I said nothing to the the *Sun* man, despite being stunned by his act of exclusion. However, Ian Herbert, a writer from the *Daily Mail*, whom I had never met before, hugged me and apologised, saying he found the moment unpalatable. He was not to blame and I welcomed his act of kindness.

Fortunately, I had my news background to fall back on and the *Evening Standard* were beginning to appreciate my talents for turning stories for them, which I was using to try and get a much-coveted staff reporter's role. This was not about money or job security. It was about foreign travel – and being accepted, something I craved. To the delight of this 25-year-old who loved the bustle and excitement of a newsroom, I was duly hired permanently, becoming the first journalist of Asian heritage in an editorial staff position on the paper.

The *Standard* had an extremely competitive newsroom staffed with some of the most brilliant journalists. They were always quick to react to breaking news. At its height the paper sold around a million copies on each weekday. I was tasked with covering murders, political stories, celebrities, the IRA attacks on London and anything anti-the Greater London Council, then the governing body for the capital.

I remember my first foreign assignment to Corfu. It was to report on a British woman who had become fond of a stray dog that had gone missing and she refused to return home with her husband when he returned to the UK.

With the help of photographer John Minihan, whose portrait of the writer Samuel Beckett taken in Paris has been described as one of the greatest photos of the twentieth century, within hours of landing we found the stray looking for scraps behind a taverna. Ah, the heady days and the big stories of 1980s Fleet Street. The dog even found TV stardom as he was airlifted to a new life in Britain and sent into quarantine before joining his new owners.

The *Evening Standard* would release four or five editions a day on to the London streets and it was thrilling to write a story at 9am and hear the print machines begin thundering away an hour later in the building – shared with the *Daily Express* – dubbed the 'Black Lubyanka' after the infamous KGB prison in Moscow. Sometimes the 'inkies' – the printers – would throw me a copy if I was too excited and too impatient to wait for the bundles in brown paper and string to be delivered to the newsroom. On occasions I would even fork out 10p on the corner of Ludgate Circus and Fleet Street if the desire to see my byline overwhelmed me. I was so delighted to be a staff reporter in Fleet Street, not least when I saw the pride on my father's face when he came into the office to greet me. It softened even the most hardened hacks to see the love my father had for me.

If it was football that had started me on my path to wanting to be a journalist, my instinct for news had a lot to do with Dad. He was always fascinated by a big news event happening in London and he would at times take me along on the old red Routemaster hop-on, hop-off buses to have a look. When President John F. Kennedy made a visit to London in 1961, Dad took me to see him and although I was too young to remember, Dad frequently told the story of how I had waved at Kennedy from my pram and shouted 'More Kennedy' as his cavalcade passed by. When I was four, Dad also took me to stand outside Buckingham Palace, though apparently I did not cover myself in glory when I was caught short and had a pee against a perimeter wall.

I have more of a memory of going, a month short of my sixth birthday, to Churchill's Hyde Park home as the ailing former Prime Minister and great leader lay dying and we joined the throng of mourners and press people outside in January 1965. I can still recall the chaplain emerging from the Churchill household and informing the crowds in barely audible tones that the great man was fading fast and that he had only hours to live. The whole drama and the tearful faces are a little hazy these days, but I remember Dad holding my hand as we boarded the bus and saying we had just witnessed the passing of a unique man and that I should try and remember I was there.

The struggle for Irish independence and the arrest of Republican activists in the 1960s saw me and Dad standing outside Shepherd's Bush police station among the waiting pressmen, him just wanting to be part of significant events. Dad also wrote letters to Enoch Powell after the 'Rivers of Blood' speech and proudly showed me the correspondence. He told me that I would find the world was full of jumped-up people and that I should always take on authority if I sensed an air of self-importance. As I did with that dodgy copper.

I witnessed Dad's dislike of bullshit politicians when he took me to the Commons late one night to sit in the Strangers' Gallery. We listened intently to some tedious debate, my eyelids practically closing, when I heard him shouting and hissing at the MPs. I never fully understood what it was that so angered my father, but he did introduce me to the Punjabi word *bakavasa* – meaning nonsense – as we walked to the bus stop through Westminster.

When the Tory leader Alec Douglas-Home was at a function, Dad and I turned up to gawp and Dad took a terrific picture of him entering the Royal Albert Hall. Also, in April 1976, we were there when Jim Callaghan became Prime Minister. In those days, the public were allowed to enter Downing Street and at the age of 17 I became a press photographer for the day. My tiny plastic 50p toy camera snapped Mr Callaghan entering Number 10 for the first time and the Prime Minister waved and smiled at me. I was practically on the doorstep and peered inside, my hands shaking at the excitement. It didn't really matter that my camera proved useless and the pictures never appeared, even though I cried and cried when I discovered how crap the camera and I had been.

It was this mix of football and news that ran through my veins and would lead me, on a hunch and with the help of a £20 return air fare, into the midst of the most sickening and traumatic of scenes, and from there, unscheduled, to covering one of the biggest, most shameful and distressing stories in English football history.

I hadn't been intending to work at the European Cup Final of 1985 between Liverpool and Juventus. The *Standard* had shown little interest in sending me as a news reporter, even though there was some history of violence between Italian and English fans and there was some talk of renewed off-field rivalries. My aim was simply to see a European final. This one not too far away in Brussels seemed like a good opportunity. The stars aligned, with the *Standard*'s sports desk at least agreeing to order a press ticket for me, and my sister Chandra Laika, who was working as cabin crew for British Airways and still is 40 years on, securing me a cheap return flight. I booked some time off from work to go.

It was a hot May afternoon in the Belgian capital when I landed and the beer was flowing in the Grand Place. I was then 26 and had never even tasted a beer. In fact, I rarely went into Fleet Street pubs, despite the drinking culture around the newspaper industry back in those days. If I did, it was to drink a cola or a fruit juice. I was astonished by the amount of drink being consumed. At first, the two sets of fans seemed to be maintaining their distance but that would change with all this alcohol on tap. Inevitably too much drink led to outbreaks of violence and I found a phone box to make a reverse-charge call to the *Standard* to file a story about windows being smashed in the Grote Markt, the Flemish name for the Grand Place. Just because I wasn't working didn't mean I wasn't working.

Of the five then paid-for editions of the *Evening Standard*, only the West End Final had not yet gone on to the machines, allowing me to make the last 100,000 copies with a few paragraphs. I thought that would be me done for the day and I could settle back and enjoy what promised to be a huge match, with Kenny Dalglish on one side and Michel Platini on the other.

Once inside the Heysel Stadium, I collected my media pass and took my allocated press seat, looking on as school children played a warm-up match as a prelude to the main event. To my left, I observed a mass of Liverpool fans occupying most of the terrace behind the goal. Next to them, separated by a flimsy fence that ran from the top of the stand to the bottom, was a supposed 'neutral' zone. It was soon evident, however, that some Italian fans had obtained neutral-area tickets and, as the kids' game carried on, missiles were being thrown between the two factions.

Soon the neutral area began to look strangely empty as fans in there scented danger from the Liverpool fans who were trying to breach the fence and get at the Juventus fans in the neutral zone, who they seemed to feel had riled them. In an attempt to escape missiles and potential oncoming attackers, the Italians and others in the zone had headed for a brick wall, where they thought they could survive the drop and get away. In the Liverpool fans' charge, though, the wall collapsed and a sickening, terrible crush ensued. As I watched it unfold, horrified, I remember the *Daily Mail*'s Jeff Powell then arriving in the press box to tell us all: 'My God, there are bodies down there.'

Instinct took me now to the area, along with all the other journalists, where the great, late *Observer* photographer Eamonn McCabe (who, despite being shell-shocked, had professionally carried on taking photographs that would later win multiple awards) guided me through the twisted metal and broken concrete. On the ground behind the stands, I saw fans sprawled. Some were still being given treatment, with efforts being made to restart their hearts. Many were clearly dead. I noticed the blue colour of one victim's face. The Liverpool chairman Sir John Smith was stunned as he walked past me and through the carnage. He had surely just been informed by the police about the growing seriousness and extent of the tragedy. Ultimately, there would be 39 people who went to a football match that night and paid with their lives.

At that moment, I thought about my own parents back in London. I pictured them in their tiny living room in Leyton, watching on television and worrying about their son. I knew I had to find a payphone to tell them I was OK. I left the scene of the story to find a kiosk. Being an evening paper, with the match happening outside their deadline, the *Standard* had had no need to order one in the press box. But it was also a means for me to escape the devastation around me. I was in panic mode. I was scared even though the mayhem was largely over. I felt I was going to be sick and that I was on the verge of collapse. Unlike some of my colleagues who seemed to be dealing professionally with the story, I was not up for these scenes of tragedy. My mother did not bring me into the world to see humans dying at at a football match.

It is still difficult to escape the visions as I write this, some 38 years later. I also have a sense of a dereliction of duty. I did not reach the professional standards that would have been expected of me. I did not carry out the necessary interviews with eyewitnesses and with those who may have lost loved ones. Even though I was not expected to file my copy until seven o'clock the next morning, there was a lot of ground I could have covered had it not been for my youth, inexperience, fright and shock. I remember nothing about the game that was somehow allowed to proceed, only that Juventus won 1-0 with a penalty for a foul that looked outside the area but which nobody seemed to have any stomach to contest. UEFA said they continued with the match because they feared violence between rival fans in the streets if it was called off.

I wandered around for several hours and in early morning I was joined by the *Evening Standard*'s chief photographer Aubrey Hart, who had taken the first flight to Brussels to cover the tragedy. We decided to head to the stadium to see what a new day's light might reveal. Typically, as if almost to affirm that Belgian police and security had been far from adequate, we were allowed to enter the crumbling old stadium and wander around the terraces – unwittingly contaminating a crime scene where the 39 had died and around 600 had been injured. I thought of the screams and the anguish of the night before as people lost their lives crushed under the bodies of their fellow supporters while much of the rest of the stadium remained in ignorance.

As we surveyed the stands where the world had witnessed the carnage only 12 hours earlier, I noticed a child's shoe among the rubble and abandoned items, crushed railings and concrete... and the tears returned. I managed to dictate a story to the *Standard*'s copytaker while trembling, and the lost shoe was a poignant, central factor of my dispatch about how the so-called 'beautiful game' had turned so intensely ugly with even children falling victim.

Eventually, 14 English football fans were convicted of involuntary manslaughter, given three-year sentences and fined around £1,000 each. Eleven others were acquitted. Some Belgian police were also punished and given suspended sentences.

To me, the sentencing of the fans was too lenient. Life sentences for murder, I believe, would have been justified. My view was deepened a few days later when I interviewed the widow of Northern Irishman Patrick Radcliffe. She told me he was not a football fan. He had been working in Brussels and was given a ticket at the last minute by a friend for the section designated for neutrals. All the deaths were tragic but there was something even more poignant about the death of someone whose first football match turned out to be his last.

Whatever anyone's opinion of Margaret Thatcher – and mine are wholly negative – there could be no contesting the Prime Minister's verdict that the Heysel Stadium violence and disaster had brought shame on the country. It would lead to English club teams being hit with a ban from the European game for five years. Official reports blamed Liverpool fans and the poor state of the stadium.

I went into my own football exile and did not attend a match for some 18 months. I was upset that, despite the ban, English football seemed to move on too quickly and violence returned. To me, football became insignificant in light of the night of horror I had witnessed, even though it meant that I missed West Ham's most successful league season in their modern history as they finished third in 1986. I plunged myself into my work instead.

In fairness, Liverpool Football Club did acknowledge the role of its fans that night and respectfully marks the anniversary each year with tributes to those who died or were injured. I, too, have never forgotten the night of 29 May 1985 – what I witnessed on the night and the morning afterwards when I went to a foreign field to celebrate life and ended up mourning death. As well as emotional scars and painful memories, it has left me with a reminder every time I go to a West Ham match, even in these days of a well-stewarded London Stadium built to high safety standards for the 2012 Olympic Games. To avoid even the potential for crowding and crushing, I go into the arena as early as possible and leave long after the final whistle.

Meera, Me and Monkey Chants

I WASN'T the only person desperate to get sight of the early editions of the *Evening Standard* back in those days.

Lines would form outside the office and wind from the Fleet Street front entrance to the bay in Shoe Lane where the vans would load the first batches of up to a million copies a day. And among the people eager to scan the ads for somewhere to live was a Manchester University drama graduate who had arrived in London from her home village near Walsall, looking for a room to rent. Her name was Meera Syal and she was to become my wife and the mother of my wonderful daughter Milli – now a talented theatre director – as well as one of Britain's best actors and writers.

The pressures of Fleet Street life made having a social life difficult, and Meera was my first serious relationship. We met in 1987 when I was 28 and she was 26. She was at a Hindu cultural event I was attending with my family on a Sunday afternoon in Peckham, south-east London, to which her Uncle Inderji had brought her, with the support of her parents, to meet an arranged-marriage candidate. In the end, to my good fortune, he hadn't turned up.

When we talked, she said she had seen my name in the *Standard* and presumed that I was a veteran correspondent in his sixties. I told her I was familiar with her work too. The very night before, indeed, she had been appearing in the West End. Now she sat here without airs or graces. I was taken by her beautiful big brown eyes and her curly hair, and especially by her genuine soft nature and her incredible wit. Nothing came of it then, but a few weeks later I was strolling down Shaftesbury Avenue with a Yorkshire lass I had been dating when I saw Meera's huge portrait outside Wyndham's Theatre, where she was starring in Caryl Churchill's play

Serious Money. I made some excuse to the Yorkshire girl about needing to be somewhere and we went our different ways – me to wait for Meera at the stage door.

She was pleased to see me again and soon we became a couple. She was especially kind to me after my mother's death that year. Within 18 months I had also lost my father, whom she had come to know and respect and who liked her too. She came to see me off at Heathrow when I flew to India to take his ashes back to immerse in the sacred River Ganges. We were married in 1989, two years after that first meeting, and it would take almost another two years before I could persuade the then love of my life to accompany me to see the love of my footballing life, to make the twain meet. The date will ever be etched on my memory: Saturday, 6 April 1991.

Meera had never been to a football match and thus not experienced the first-hand racism that I had growing up in the East End as a Hammers fan – including from my own club's supporters – but she had certainly noted it, in the monkey chants coming through her television screen and the callous treatment of black footballers in the 1970s and 1980s. She had been born in the West Midlands coal-mining village of Essington, her family the only people of colour there, and her wonderful parents Surendra and Surinder had done their best to shield her from the harsh realities of racism (in the area where Enoch Powell was an MP and stoked division) that they had faced when they arrived in Britain at the end of the 1950s. She had told me, for example, during the early days of our relationship how as a little girl she had fallen over in her school playground and grazed her knee. Her schoolmates could not hide their amazement when her blood turned out to be red. It was a moment that would always stay with her.

She grew up to become an astonishingly bright young woman who declined the invitation to go to Oxbridge because she wanted to study in a diverse city and university. She chose Manchester, where she was awarded a double first in English and Drama. When we met, she was establishing herself as a writer and actor and was on the verge of joining the excellent black cast of the BBC's comedy series *The Real McCoy*. She had won the *Sunday Times* best newcomer award at the Edinburgh Festival at the age of 22 for her play *One of Us*.

She soon shared her passion for theatre with me and introduced me to the plays of Shakespeare, Ibsen and Arthur Miller. In turn I wanted her to love football so much. But she was wary. And her reticence would be reinforced when on our wedding day – 15 April 1989 – we were both shaken in learning of the Hillsborough disaster at the FA Cup semi-final between Liverpool and Nottingham Forest with the loss of 97 lives via our chauffeur's car radio as we were driven from our wedding in Lichfield to the reception. The newsman in me nearly kicked in when I thought I was probably an hour away at most, but I kept quiet and gave my undivided attention to my beautiful bride.

Though her brother Rajeev (who would go on to become home affairs editor for *The Guardian*) was a Wolverhampton Wanderers fan, Meera's family were more about musical evenings and family gatherings. Her father was a wonderful singer. She was apprehensive about the anger of a white football terrace. I tried to tell her that only a small minority of people who went to football were capable of being racist. The majority were decent and, indeed, behaved decently. Finally she agreed to come to a match with me on that April Saturday in 1991.

We had gone to Walsall for the weekend to spend time with her parents and I'd bought two tickets for West Ham's game some 40 miles north up the M6 in Burslem against Port Vale. I really wanted to go with the Hammers – then under club legend Billy Bonds' management – fighting for promotion back to the First Division. We would be seated, I told Meera. She agreed, albeit a little reluctantly, and so we set off for her very first match. I hadn't told her that our seats, above the tunnel, were among the home fans. As we sat down, I jokingly told her that in the unlikely event of West Ham scoring, we would have to feign disappointment to blend in with the Port Vale supporters.

All was going well until a local Neanderthal decided that he would put his hands under his armpits and make monkey noises each time West Ham's black midfielder George Parris touched the ball. When it continued, Meera realised that I was about to lose it and she gripped my hand tightly. I could see she was as disgusted as I was but she didn't want any trouble.

It was when the same bloke created a funnel with his hands and chanted 'Ooh-ooh-ooh' even more loudly at Parris that I finally flipped. The player was about 50 metres away and thankfully wouldn't have heard the insults being thrown his way but Meera and I did. I politely asked the dumbass if he wouldn't mind refraining from such cretinous behaviour. His response was to insist that he could say what he liked and to point out that we shouldn't have been there in the first place. I whispered to Meera that he probably meant we shouldn't be in the Port Vale seats, but she asked me how he could be sure we were not also supporting Port Vale. It was a good question. We weren't wearing West Ham colours and had not been cheering for them.

I looked around at the sea of white faces and nobody else was saying anything to stop this numbskull. Most people looked away. Some smirked as if they condoned his behaviour. Now, I hadn't had a fight since the school playground, but it did cross my mind to maybe stick one on him. Fear kicked in, though, particularly for my wife's safety. Instead, I thought about leaving and getting her out of there.

Half-time came and with the score at 0-0, I realised we hadn't really taken much notice of the football. When I looked into Meera's eyes as she clutched my arm tightly, I knew I had to do something. Nothing macho, but something to keep the idiot in check and ensure he was the one who didn't resort to violence. But what?

A uniformed police officer appeared from a stairwell and I took my chance, leaving my seat to tell him of the offensive chanting we had witnessed. I expected him to seek to persuade me to ignore the abuse – perhaps to treat it as banter, and to try and enjoy the game – as I had little faith in people understanding how much offence and hurt such racist behaviour caused to such as me and my wife. Instead, I was surprised to hear the policeman tell me that the behaviour was not acceptable and that he would have a word with Mr Racist. The officer accompanied me back to our seats and pointedly told him: 'Any repeat of this and you will be arrested. These people have as much right to enjoy the football as you, so shut up!' He then turned to me and Meera and told us that if there was any repeat, he would be nicking the bloke, adding – as he saw the stress in our eyes – 'And to make sure, I'm going to stand right here for the rest of the match. You'll both be alright now.'

True to his word, the officer stood steadfastly and reassuringly near us, his eyes glancing from the pitch to us and on to the offender. I can recall it reaffirming our faith in our country that most people, police included, believed in fair play. As for the match, however, it became difficult to enjoy. Unable to relax into it, our eyes turned often to the policeman and the racist whose fury was obvious despite his silence. It was satisfying, though, when Ian Bishop curled a shot into the Port Vale net to give us the points. I wished we'd been able to stand up and celebrate. To have done so might have seen our 'friend' unable to control his seething silence. Meera was largely silent on the drive back down the M6. I was racked with guilt and blamed myself for putting her in that situation. It was a day of menace that she did not need.

Our marriage ended soon after the millennium, after 13 years. But she remains my best friend and has given me the most precious gift of a darling daughter, Milli. Meera is the most humble, creative and giving woman I have ever met. She is a fantastic role model for young artistes and has had to work twice as hard to be allowed to fill the roles that have made her a household name as well as write them herself. I am proud of her wonderful theatre and TV work for which she has been awarded a CBE. Barrie Keeffe, the late writer of the film *The Long Good Friday*, once said in a radio interview that Meera would become the first Asian dame of the British theatre. That cannot be too far off and I was delighted to read in *The Times* that Elizabeth II had once described *The Kumars at No. 42* as her favourite TV programme and was even able to recite some of the one-liners from the grandma character, which Meera played and created. (Granny Kumar's appearance was based on an elderly member of the family. But that remains our secret.)

Meera later married her co-star of the *Goodness Gracious Me* comedy series, Sanjeev Bhaskar, who is a Liverpool supporter and is invited to Anfield as a guest. She, however, will not go, despite having the chance of a safe, luxury seat. Indeed, she has never been to another football match, and we have never spoken of our sorrowful experience at Port Vale again.

Therein lies my sadness. Meera is a strong feminist, a brave and intelligent woman who has had many battles against racial inequality and actively campaigns against violence towards women. She has become probably Britain's most famous Asian woman. But if she can be put off from football, how many more women and people of colour hold back from involvement? That, at the very least, should have the footballing authorities sitting up and taking note.

The Bowyer Insult

IF SOMEBODY, even someone as strong as Ms Meera Syal, can be deterred from just *watching* the game, what might it be like for young players of Asian heritage who would like to be playing it? What might they have to endure? How many Asian parents keep their children from going to matches, let alone encourage them to enter it as a profession?

There have certainly been very few who have made it through into the professional ranks, and even fewer who have appeared in the Premier League. Those who spring to mind are Harpal Singh, who started at Leeds United, Zesh Rehman of Fulham and Michael Chopra of Sunderland, all of whom are pioneers I have interviewed. More recently there is Hamza Choudhury of Leicester City. Yet – unlike the vast numbers of Afro-Caribbean kids who have lit up the English game over the last 50 years, following in the footsteps of brave, racially abused trailblazers like Viv Anderson, the first black man to play for England – the few Asian role models have not been successful in drawing young Asian men and women into the sport. Nobody seems to have been able to come up with a single, defining reason why it has never happened the way it has for black players. We're still not seeing much of an influx even though racism is less overt in the game.

Despite the lack of Asian representation on professional football pitches, Sunny Singh Gill made Premier League history and a major breakthrough by refereeing the match between Crystal Palace and Luton at Selhurst Park in the March of the 2023/24 season. There are also three sets of Asian owners of English clubs in Shahid Khan at Fulham, Shilen Patel at West Bromwich Albion and India's VH Group, through the Venky family, at Blackburn Rovers. Their financial backing has bafflingly yet to yield star south Asian players, however.

It is something I have discussed with Sanjay Bhandari, MBE, chairman of the football organisation Kick It Out, who has been a friend for more than 35 years. A lifelong Manchester United fan, Sanjay believes there are a multitude of reasons why Asians are not more prominent in the national game. He says stereotyping and the attitudes of coaches and scouts are a problem, with the misguided perception that Asians are smaller and less physical and have poorer diets. He also says that Asians are on the outside of the footballing community looking in and that there needs to be at least a 5 per cent target in clubs' academy systems.

There are jokes and stereotypes about Asian kids being needed to help in the family's corner shop after school and at weekends, precluding them from playing football, but there is some truth in it. I remember on Saturdays having to help my dad with his work, lugging items from his warehouse on public transport for him. I had to miss watching or playing sometimes – and I was a football-daft kid. Family time, eating and doing things together, is hugely important in Asian families, and it is true in many cases that parents want their kids to go into 'professions', like banking and the law, as my father did with me. There is loyalty, and unity and dedication to each other's welfare, rather than the individualism and dedication – of time and approach – that exists in other communities. John Terry's mum, Sue, told me that he and his brother Paul used to play a game after school, come home for a bite to eat and to pick up clean kit then train or play again the same evening. More at weekends. I could never envisage my parents tolerating and supporting that.

When it comes to the dearth of Asian-heritage supporters, not much has changed there either. In January 2024, at the match between West Ham and Bournemouth, I discovered by chance that seated three rows away from me in the Billy Bonds stand at the London Stadium was a Mr Rajat Bhatia. We got chatting and discovered that we are distantly related, although had only once before met at a family funeral. Now we were two brown faces in a sea of white ones, both loving the claret and blue. As we sank £7 pints of Italian beer at half-time, Rajat asked me: 'Uncle: [he is nearly 30 years younger] there are no other Indians here… why do you think that is?' Half-time did not last long enough, but it struck me that this fine talented gentleman from

India, who has lived in Britain for almost ten years and been attending West Ham home matches for several years, had also been bothered by the lack of diversity on the terraces without some of the more unpalatable experiences of yesteryear.

To answer his question, I firmly believe racism still festers on the terraces and social media has given it a new channel. It is understandably off-putting; being a person of colour among thousands of white fans screaming at the pitch and wondering if the anger might be turned against you can be a solitary experience. Even though the game is lucky enough to have a good number of black players, to my mind it still hasn't manifested in comparable numbers of black fans taking a place in the stands. Whenever I scan those stands, either in person or on television, I can still spot black fans because there are so few and it cheers me to see them celebrating along with fellow supporters.

West Ham are trying, it has to be acknowledged. Playing legend Mark Noble, now the club's sporting director, has offered encouraging words on how he would like to see a player of south Asian background star for the team and he and the club, via the 'Emerging Hammers' programme, are reaching into the boroughs of Newham, Tower Hamlets, Redbridge, Barking and Dagenham, and Havering, which contain 325,000 people of south Asian heritage. Youth football teams with larger numbers of Asian players are being welcomed into the fold.

There is also the 'Inclusive Irons' group of West Ham south Asian fans, whom I first encountered on the streets of Frankfurt in 2022 and who remained cheerful despite having just seen the team knocked out of the Europa Cup semi-final by Eintracht. They speak out against racism and discourage West Ham fans from racist chanting. The West Ham women's team have also given grounds for optimism with the Indian national team's goalkeeper Aditi Chauhan on their books for three years. (Coincidentally she was a pupil at Delhi's Amity International School where another relative, Divya Bhatia, is the headtcacher and remembers her well.)

In addition, the FA have tried many initiatives and there is progress, even if I do wonder sometimes whether racist attitudes have been suppressed rather than changed. I dream that one day I will see a turbaned youngster in West Ham colours being carried around Wembley by his team-mates after scoring an FA Cup Final winner. I hope he bhangras across the pitch too in celebration.

Any hope of that was probably set back a whole generation when, early in the 2000s, an unhappy episode saw the club undo a lot of good work that was also going on back then to banish the race-hate brigade. They had similarly been making all the right noises in trying to entice the vast Asian community around Upton Park to come to the Boleyn Ground, even if it felt like a long job with my Asian brothers and sisters still not coming to games in any real numbers. For many of us, it is not a big social occasion with plenty of drinking before and after. Those like me who do attend, are not seen in the bars around grounds. It's that family thing again; they want to be home with kin as much as possible.

I recall Roger Morgan, one of the footballing twins who played for QPR and Spurs, also going into Newham's schools and classrooms as the club's community official at that time to encourage Asian kids to feel they might belong. But his and the club's honest endeavours fell largely on deaf ears. It seemed that wounds were deep. This was a club, after all, that had attracted the most vicious racists and had even secretly invited the Rhodesian Prime Minister Ian Smith into the ground in the 1970s.

I'd kept the faith, remaining loyal, and would travel up and down the country to support the team. I had even followed them to Holland for a series of pre-season friendlies. On the rare occasion when I would see a person of colour at the Boleyn, my smile of solidarity would be as wide as Green Street. All my goodwill and warmth towards West Ham disappeared, however, in January 2003 when the club signed the midfield player Lee Bowyer from Leeds United. Three years earlier, he and team-mate Jonathan Woodgate had been charged with causing grievous bodily harm to a young Asian student who had been attacked near a nightclub. Woodgate was convicted of affray, and Bowyer was cleared but he would agree an out-of-court settlement in 2005 of £170,000 in a civil case for damages brought by the victim and his brother, who was less seriously hurt. Bowyer was also fined by Leeds for his role in events.

I felt the whole thing stank, not least because the case was heard by an all-white jury. What didn't come out in court was the fact that in 1996, shortly after his move from Charlton Athletic to Leeds, Bowyer was caught on video, with two friends, throwing chairs at two Asian staff at a McDonald's on the Isle of Dogs in east London. One of the Asian lads suffered a bruised head and cuts and grazes; the other had bruising and a cut on his scalp that needed five stitches. Bowyer admitted affray, was fined £4,500 and ordered to pay £175 to the two victims. Leeds United also fined Bowyer £4,000 and warned him that a repetition could result in his being sold. Magistrates told the footballer they had nearly jailed him for his part in the 'disgraceful incident'.

I felt let down by my club and, although I knew anything I said or did was probably not going to make any difference to them signing him, I had to speak out. When *The Guardian* and the *Daily Mirror* approached me to write about it all for them, and BBC and ITV asked me to appear, I was only too willing. It probably all came spilling out most vividly in *The Guardian*:

Like bad old Alf Garnett and his claret and blue West Ham scarf, miserable memories are being evoked once again. It is bad enough that they are at the basement of the Premiership but today, at a stroke and before the ink is dry on the contract Lee Bowyer will sign, West Ham will risk consigning years of good work in furthering relations with Newham's Asian community to the dustbin.

As an Asian, an East Ender and a supporter of West Ham for more than 30 years, it is difficult to find sense in the move they are embarking on to ensure Premiership survival. Even though there are not that many supporters like me in London E13, I can only survey the signing of Bowyer as an Asian. It stinks.

My opposition to Bowyer is so strong that it supersedes the fight to stay in the top flight and the importance of being able to see the likes of Beckham and Rooney over Ince and the other has-beens.

In welcoming Bowyer, West Ham are closing the door on Newham's vast Asian population – who admittedly have hardly beaten a well-worn path through the Bobby Moore gates.

I still shake when I recall the vile practice of Paki-bashing in the 1970s. The sight of the boot-boys used to make me run for cover on the old Chicken Run. I missed many goals while hiding behind the stand.

I was a scared and helpless schoolboy, caught up in the magic of West Ham's free-flowing play. My admiration for the gentleman Bobby Moore and his fellow World Cup winners was overpowering. I didn't want to go into law like my father and his father, I wanted to be carried off the pitch on the shoulders of my team-mates having scored the winning goal in injury-time and brought West Ham the First Division championship trophy.

And in any case, were not West Ham at the forefront of pioneering the employment of black players? We had Clyde Best and Ade Coker. That said a lot more to me than any of those morons who would show off their braces and bootlaces and abuse elderly Asian women along Green Street.

In many ways it is different now. The skinheads have long gone and so have any other dim-witted, low-IQ racists. They have been marginalised and the elderly women who attend the Upton Park market on Saturday-afternoon match days rarely suffer abuse.

Now Bowyer is set to line up in claret and blue and it is a huge step backwards for the club. There are not even any footballing arguments in his favour. We already have Joe Cole and Michael Carrick.

My main worry is that the signing of Bowyer will appeal to those racists who have long been marginalised. They may feel that the time is right to return to the terraces.

West Ham must not look at damage-limitation now. Of prime importance is that young Asians are not put off even more from coming into the ground. Glenn Roeder has to speak out against racism and not ignore the baggage that comes with Bowyer. It cannot be ignored.

If Bowyer can bring himself to do it, he should be encouraged to acknowledge the importance of the Asian community in Newham to West Ham and how wrong it is to hurl abuse and chairs at young Asians trying to make a few quid working at east London's McDonald's restaurants. He needs to say racism is not nice. It could help him, too.

It won't shift my opinion of him. I will not be able to hand over my £40 per game knowing that some of it will line his pocket. I wish West Ham all the success we have craved since 1980. But I won't be able to bring myself to see the Hammers play while Bowyer stands there. I hope his residency in London E13 is a short one.

The *Mirror* editor Piers Morgan gave me the biggest picture byline over two days and allowed me to pontificate on the sports pages even further. There was a long headline reading:

No member of an ethnic minority will want to sign for them. No Asian will want to support them. That's how taking on Lee Bowyer harms West Ham.

Beneath it, I wrote:

As a West Ham supporter for more than 30 years – and the proud owner of season ticket 00001 in the club's centenary season – the proposed signing of Lee Bowyer breaks my heart.

As an Asian East Ender, I have put up with years of criticism from my friends about supporting a club like West Ham, who hardly had the best community relations in the seventies in the era of Paki-bashing.

I remember I used to shudder with fear when the boot boys would march past me on the section of Upton Park then known as the Chicken Run.

Alf Garnett also conspired to make my life a misery. Here was an out-and-out racist who wore a West Ham scarf and swore loyalty to Bobby Moore.

Perhaps screenwriters in 2003, were they writing a new series of the BBC 'comedy', might replace Garnett's target of affection of the great gentleman and legend Moore with the sneering Bowyer.

Now 30 years later, arrives Bowyer. A man convicted of outrageous behaviour for hurling abuse and chairs at Asian staff at a McDonald's restaurant.

Over the years the morons who used to plague the Hammers have been largely marginalised.

But in Bowyer there is a danger they could find the perfect excuse to return to Upton Park unless he makes public statements distancing himself from such vile people.

He has to go on record and make clear he abhors racism and understands why West Ham needs its Asian community.

But I am afraid for me, the signing of Lee Bowyer is a step too far. I can no longer bring myself to fork out £40 and walk through the turnstiles to see Bowyer playing in claret and blue.

I would just rather Bowyer kissed my brown arse and disappeared back to Elland Road.

We do not need him and as long as he is at Upton Park, I assume the club does not need me.

On reflection, I probably shouldn't have asked Bowyer to kiss my backside. That was a crass remark. But such was my anger and frustration. In the end, he played only 11 times for the Hammers as they were relegated. I felt no sympathy for him with all his injuries and I admired the West Ham fans who protested against his signing. My resentment against him was deepened many years later when I discovered that he had only signed a six-month contract on his first stay at the club. We were a stopover, a place for him to get fit, on his way to Newcastle.

Even though Bowyer was long gone, it took me a couple of years to find the enthusiasm to watch the team live again. Thankfully, my anger had subsided enough for me to attend the 2006 FA Cup Final against Liverpool with my fellow West Ham sufferer and mate Danny Groom. We were close enough to hear Paul Konchesky's squeals of delight when his cross from the byline flew over goalkeeper Pepe Reina and into the net in the 64th minute to give West Ham a 3-2 lead. It lasted until injury time, when Steven Gerrard fired home from 35 yards and his team went on to lift the trophy after a penalty shoot-out. A month or so later, I found myself in Baden-Baden covering the World Cup, standing next to Gerrard and looking down at his right foot, lamenting what it had done to my team.

Losing in an FA Cup Final, despite the heartbreak it caused for many weeks after, was no great shame, though. That came with the return of Bowyer a few months later in 2006. I was astonished when the divisive character signed again and West Ham compounded their crass move of a few years before. He had not long before disgraced Newcastle's colours by engaging in an on-pitch brawl with team-mate Kieron Dyer in a Premier League match against Aston Villa. Though Bowyer landed the first punch, both received red cards and were banned for three games. The FA saw who the more errant player was, however, and fined Bowyer £30,000, imposing an additional three-game ban. Newcastle fined him six weeks' wages while the Northumbria police charged him in connection with the brawl under Section 4 of the Public Order Act. He admitted the lesser charge of using threatening behaviour and was fined £600 and ordered to pay £1,000 in costs.

As I read about his arrest, I felt my opposition to him had been justified. I hadn't forgiven West Ham for signing him first time around, but to re-sign him was an even more bitter blow. Back in 2003, I had found Bowyer's time at West Ham repulsive and offensive. Now to welcome him back as some type of long-lost prodigal son was nothing short of stomach-churning. I could not understand what the directors at the club were thinking after all the efforts to bring more Asians through the turnstiles. Friends tried to persuade me Bowyer deserved a second chance, but I was not about to cheer him or put money into his pocket. I had enjoyed returning to the club and sitting behind Alan Pardew's dugout after Bowyer had left but that would not be happening again. I resolved to go into exile from the Boleyn until Bowyer was gone. It would be a long two and a half years, but for my personal integrity, it had to be done.

As for the club, almost 18 years later I was forced to question their attitudes once more. All these local initiatives and cheerful articles on their website about involvement with east London's Asian community and I turn up at the London Stadium for a match against Aston Villa to find, to my disgust, a glossy feature about Bowyer in the matchday programme lauding his time at the club with a photo of him in West Ham shirt, arms raised as if in celebration. The pain returned.

Corruption in Zurich

BY THE time of the Bowyer period, I was a freelance, with a seven-year spell at the *Daily* and *Sunday Express* behind me following an unhappy ending to my career at the *Evening Standard*. It had been simmering for a long while as I came to discover that racism was in journalism as well as football.

For many years I sought to shrug it off and get on with the job I loved, but in the end it made me dread going into the office, which led to a colleague, Richard Littlejohn – who would go on to be the *Daily Mail*'s star columnist – nicknaming me Shergar because I would go missing for so long. He was unaware, like many friends, of the racism and pain I endured.

When I married Meera, the same news executive who had uttered a racist slur against black people at an office Christmas party in my presence asked me with a look of disdain: 'I suppose you'll be having children, then?' The subtext to me was clear from the look on his face: so you'll be bringing more Asians into the world, then? That was the start of comments and treatment that, to some people, may not sound too shocking at first hearing but that are persistent and draining. While some colleagues may have been accepting of me, there was a fair bit of hurtful racism in what was a very busy newsroom, full of hard drinkers and huge egos. In fact, there was no culture of kindness – far from it. It was like being back on the terraces at West Ham as a kid; you were excited to be there but always looking over your shoulder. A dream and a nightmare at the same time.

In the *Daily Mirror* newsroom in the 1980s a senior journalist had branded me a 'monkey' and asked: 'Who cut your fucking tree down?' He'd had a drink, of course, and for fear of upsetting my paymasters, I let it pass. Another *Mirror* colleague branded me their 'sepoy runner', which is the term of reference used by the British Army for an Indian soldier serving under their orders.

I vividly recall one episode while reporting for the *Evening Standard* that upset me, in late September of 1993 when I was in Brighton covering the Labour Party Conference and an email dropped into the computer of a colleague seated beside me. He started to laugh and I leant over to read the email.

'Sir Colin Powell... the nights/Knights are getting darker,' it said. It was a reference to news breaking that the United States Secretary of State Colin Powell was to be made an Honorary Knight Commander of the Order of the Bath. It may have been a simple attempt at humour, what the sender thought was some smart-arse pun on night and knight, but it was ill-judged and reminded me of the venom that lay behind the treatment I had been receiving – the last to be sent on coveted foreign assignments and the first to be rung in the early hours to head to some nasty doorstep. Some of my supposed superiors just could not accept me as I was: a man with brown skin from the East End. But I had made it to Fleet Street with sheer hard work and no part in any white or old boys' network.

Despite some people's desire to drag me down, I was living the dream. I did make a complaint about this racist 'joke' to an executive, who duly took me for tea and cake and sweet-talked me out of making my anger official.

I continued to try and get assigned to sporting events and managed to make the Wimbledon tennis fortnight 'my own', being congratulated by colleagues for the stories I turned out. I was also sent to the 1988 European Football Championship in West Germany and met my idol Sir Trevor Brooking, who was commentating for the BBC. Mind you, I had to endure two sports reporters among the travelling pack telling me they felt that the National Front had some valid points to make. They were a different pair from the two tennis writers at the All England Tennis and Croquet Club one year who seemed to think it was OK to use the N-word in front of me. Hunched over their computers, they were discussing how a 'n***er like MaliVai Washington' had made it to the Wimbledon final. I gave them an ear-bashing, as a result of which neither spoke to me again, something for which I was grateful.

In 1993, I stuck my neck out and volunteered to interview the British National Party candidate for the Millwall ward of Tower Hamlets Council, Derek Beackon. Little was known about him except that he had a Hitler-like moustache and was a proud supporter of far-right ideology. I travelled to Stepney to meet him. For some reason, the paper had told his aides the reporter would be called Greg. When I emerged from my car, Beackon looked shocked and stumbled backwards into the road. After some preamble he agreed to give me 'two minutes' in a pavement interview, but what followed was a racist diatribe that had him projecting spittle in my face. When I tried to change the subject and said it might be better to talk about issues like the rubbish on the streets, he smirked and said: 'The Asians are the rubbish on the streets.' (That line about Asians being rubbish was later studied by a young and angry Sikh student called Amar Singh, who would tell me that he decided on reading it that he wanted to enter journalism. He became editor of *Eastern Eye* and went on to join the *Standard*.)

I filed my story, but I was angry that it didn't appear on the day of the election. When I queried it, the *Evening Standard* newsdesk ran it the next day as a piece informing people about the man who had been elected by just seven votes to become the BNP's first ever councillor. My story was a single column, almost a sop to me. At the top was a picture of me and Beackon, him smirking and me distressed. The then editor of the *Standard*, Stewart Steven, approached me in the newsroom to apologise and shake my hand. He said as a Jew he didn't want to risk any accusation of bias, but added that he had made a mistake and the story should have run on the day Tower Hamlets residents went to the polls to warn them of the bigot standing for election and his views of that borough's vast Asian population. Too late.

I was disillusioned by the episode and – coupled with the racist references and the self-importance and clear prejudices of a handful of executives – I knew my time at the paper had to end, even though the *Evening Standard* was a thoroughly professional outfit, staffed by the best reporters, photographers, editors, sub-editors, desk people and administrative staff. How we churned out five newspapers full of quality each day and evening still fills me with excited wonderment.

I quit in early 1994 to join the *Daily Express* and went on to news edit and be the showbusiness editor with a team of ten. I also became chief reporter of the *Sunday Express*. The organisation was clearly fading through a lack of investment and running well behind its major rival the *Daily Mail*, but it battled away the best it could.

One of the appeals of the *Express* for me was more foreign and sporting assignments. Among the first was a trip to Trinidad to try and find Brian Lara's 'secret' girlfriend. Thankfully his mother Pearl was very helpful and invited me in to her home in Santa Cruz. It enabled me to get some great copy and compete with the *Mail*, who had 'bought up' the great West Indian cricketer. The front-page story had the headline 'Tell Lara I love him'.

I was also allowed to report on Euro '96 and was inside Wembley for that Gazza goal against Scotland and Stuart Pearce's redemption against Spain. The France World Cup of 1998 followed, along with the magical 2000 Sydney Olympics, which provided me with probably my greatest sporting moment: when Cathy Freeman won the 400 metres, the Aboriginal carrying the dreams of her fellow indigenous peoples and the hopes of other Australians who rallied behind her and hoped it could ease collective national guilt and help with recognition of the immense ill treatment of its First People.

The biggest news story of my career was – and remains – the death of the Princess of Wales in Paris, and I was in the French capital within hours of the shocking road crash that claimed two other lives. Despite my two decades of newspaper experience, it was still difficult to know where to start when stepping off the Eurostar at the Gare du Nord. I felt huge sadness as I watched the then Prince Charles and Princess Diana's two older sisters accompany the casket home the day after the tragedy. A few weeks later I met Mr Nelson Mandela while on a royal trip to South Africa with the prince and his son Harry, who just looked lost to the world. My heart broke for him.

In between, I was sent to Kolkata to cover the death of Mother Teresa, with the words of the foreign editor in my ear: 'Well, having buried one saint, you can fuck off to Calcutta and bury another... Mother Teresa has died.' My life had gone full circle. Some 20 years earlier I had written to the *Evening Standard* letters pages, primarily as a teenager desperate to see his name in print, praising Mother Teresa on winning the Nobel Peace Prize. I had ended my letter with the words: 'Mother Teresa – I touch your feet.' (A Hindu means of showing respect to elders.) Inside St Thomas Church in Calcutta, staring at her corpse clad in a blue and white sari, I noticed her feet. They were within touching distance, and for the first time I recalled that letter and my desire to show my respects came into my memory. Before I knew it, my hands were out of my pockets and about to reach over the rope to her feet when I was abruptly stopped by an armed guard who sternly shouted 'Sir!'

I was also sent to the States to cover Michael Douglas and Catherine Zeta-Jones's wedding and got to speak to Kirk Douglas. I told him that watching him in the film *Ace in the Hole,* about a reporter who went to any lengths to get a story, had helped further my interest in becoming a journalist as a kid. 'Yeah,' he replied, 'you and a million others.'

I left the *Express* titles in May 2001, gratefully accepting a redundancy cheque after the papers had been taken over by a new proprietor in Richard Desmond, and for the next 14 years – until *Mail Online* hired me as their senior reporter and placed me in New York – I was a freelance. I managed to travel to four World Cups – in Japan, Germany, South Africa and Brazil – and covered three more Olympic Games, in Athens, Beijing and London. There were also more Wimbledon Championships, Test cricket and even NBA in San Antonio, Texas. I also improved my tennis and made TV documentaries for the UK and America.

I did apply for a couple of high-profile jobs during that period, as sports editor of the *Financial Times* and as an on-air sports correspondent for BBC TV. I got down to the final two for the *FT* post and had a good conversation with my interviewer about stories I'd like to cover, including ones that might go on the front page even though they didn't have a financial angle. They were very receptive... unlike the BBC, where I was almost straight away asked to do a piece to camera although I'd had no training. I was a story-getter not a polished TV pro and would have needed time in the job and practice in the classroom or studio. The process was conducted by a group of BBC executives and it didn't go well. To be honest, I think the Beeb were just box-ticking. The organisation has made progress in its diversity and hiring of people of colour but it still needs to look at who gets the top jobs rather than focusing on those starting out.

Thankfully, I had a decent name in national papers and could deliver good stories. I would even one year be shortlisted for the Asian Media Awards Sports Journalist of the Year (I didn't win). During the black-tie dinner in Manchester, I received a tip that Wayne Rooney would be painting park benches at 7am in the city as part of his community service for drink-driving. I doubted it. I knew Rooney was at Stamford Bridge playing for Everton in their Carabao Cup match with Chelsea that night and would not be back until the early hours. I rocked up anyway with a photographer in the dark and in freezing temperatures and was staggered to see Rooney emerge and walking through the mist to accept his punishment before breakfast time. He thought about putting up his hood when he saw us but accepted that we'd found him.

And so I was often able as a freelance to pick and choose my assignments and was in some demand. Amid it all came a chilly early December day in Switzerland in 2010, when I saw that it was not just racism that was rife in both journalism and football, but that corruption was also endemic to the game. It was the day when England made its final push to host the World Cup finals of 2018.

With few flights taking off from a snowbound London, I'd been fortunate to make it to the announcement at FIFA headquarters in Zurich. In fact, the previous day, my plane had been cancelled. This time, ground crew spent hours removing ice from the wings. Only a few British newspaper journalists had made it to Switzerland, among them a colleague from the *Daily Star*. We had a pint together and agreed that football was finally coming home. This was because we were picking up positive vibes from the England camp, which had David Beckham, Prime Minister David Cameron and Prince William in the entourage. Beckham and the prince had been presented as England's poster boys for the bid and I saw Cameron smiling broadly later that night as he skipped out of a back door with his communications chief – Andy Coulson, former editor of the *News of the World* – to their waiting chauffeur, the job seemingly done.

It was going to be the result of 24 hours' intense lobbying and royal hand-shaking as England laid out plans to stage the best World Cup ever. Prince William told his audience: 'I stand here before you as president of the English Football Association. Football is England's national game. It's part of the fabric of our nation. Today it is a supremely powerful force, binding the country together. It unites people of all ages, all walks of life. It's a passion. I love football. We English love football. That's why it would be such an honour to host the 2018 FIFA World Cup. But it's not just about us – England is committed to developing football internationally as a member of your football family.'

I also witnessed how Beckham had presented the suits with his most charming side – charm I had witnessed at the 2002 World Cup when the reception he received by fans outside the England team hotels was akin to Beatlemania and thousands of young Japanese boys had even copied his Mohican hairstyle. I also was there in Singapore in

2005 to see the stardust my fellow Leytonstone lad sprinkled on London's successful bid for the 2012 Olympic Games. Bringing the global football icon and all the glitter that went with him to Zurich was a masterstroke, applauded by many. Clearly coached and well versed on his presentation to FIFA, Beckham told them his grandfather Joe had died exactly a year to the day when he was in South Africa helping make the 2010 World Cup draw. 'Now I want to do something that will make my grandad proud,' he said. 'Now I want to do more... The benefits will be felt over generations and your vote can make this happen. To create a better future for our grandchildren and many millions more, just imagine what we can achieve together. Our dream is to stage a World Cup that benefits billions, that makes you, your grandchildren and everyone in football truly proud.'

I sipped a £5 coffee, convinced that the 22 FIFA delegates would select England over Russia, joint bidders Belgium and Netherlands, and Spain and Portugal. Why, we were told that FIFA vice-president Jack Warner had even put his arm around Prince William and said: 'You have my vote.' I even began to have dreams of a West Ham captain lifting the World Cup again, this time in the form of Mark Noble, who I couldn't quite believe had never even won a full England cap. I was reliably informed that when Noble was in his prime, the then England manager Roy Hodgson preferred Jonjo Shelvey to our one-club hero.

Then came the result of the ballot. England received just two votes in the first round and were eliminated. Two?! What had happened there? Russia, with 13 of the 22 votes, were awarded the tournament after the second round. Our confidence was ludicrously misplaced. Either the FA and their media people were being given duplicitous information or they had totally misread the signals. I lean towards the first explanation.

Soon my report was leading the front page of that night's *Evening Standard* – my old employers who had hired me to go to Zurich as a freelance – alongside a picture of a glum Prince William:

England's dream of bringing football home after 52 years was shattered today as Russia were chosen to host the 2018 World Cup.

> Prince William, in the city to support England's bid, looked devastated and closed his eyes as the result was declared.

The result stank, but the proceedings were to get even more bizarre a few minutes after the Russian delegation, which included the former Arsenal star Andrey Arshavin, had been feted and invited to lift the World Cup on the stage. The FIFA president Sepp Blatter opened the second envelope to reveal that Qatar would host the 2022 tournament. Qatar had never even played in a World Cup but they had beaten off the challenge of the United States, who had flown in Bill Clinton to promote their bid.

I could feel the shock around the room at both Russia and Qatar being chosen, but it seemed barely to register with the self-satisfied FIFA top brass seated in the front rows alongside Chelsea's Russian owner Roman Abramovich and the emir and sheikhs of Qatar. I had noticed the great French midfield player Zinedine Zidane, who had been brought in by Qatar, smiling like the cat that got the cream – that and quite probably a few riyals too for his role as an ambassador.

It felt to me, and many others there that day, that money was the ruling reason for the decisions. That would be confirmed years later after intensive investigations that saw the United States Department of Justice prove that representatives working for Russia and Qatar – two countries with abominable human rights records – had bribed FIFA officials to secure their bids.

The then mayor of London, Boris Johnson, was left shocked as well, lamenting: 'We put together a cracking bid, our technical specification was top notch and our stadiums would have been packed to the rafters. Londoners love football. This is a blow.' Personally, I could not resist some joshing with him, though, as I have for many years enjoyed winding up politicians. Having met him several times before, he recognised me as a reporter when I approached him outside in the sub-zero temperatures and snow. Dressed in woolly bobble hat, he was accompanied by his top aide, Guto Harri. Both were checking their phones and googling the weather in London. On seeing me, Johnson said: 'I'm in a lot of trouble, aren't I?' My reply – 'I think you probably are' – brought a rakish smile from the future prime minister. London was at a standstill and struggling because of the Arctic conditions and here was its mayor away on what was to be a pointless exercise, searching the internet for the capital's weather update.

While he and the official England party departed, reporters were advised to stay on because a mystery VIP guest would be addressing us. Dozens of armed plain-clothed bodyguards were arriving, scoping an already secure venue and flexing their muscles. Soon, President Vladimir Putin, grinning and grandstanding, walked into the room. That was, indeed, a short haul from Moscow. It was more likely that he had been circling Swiss airspace with his security detail or had even arrived earlier, tipped off that Russia would win. Nobody believed him when he said he had no idea that Russia had won until the result had been announced. He tried to lighten the tension by talking about Roman Abramovich, saying: 'Maybe he can give us some money.' The BBC's former sports editor Mihir Bose, sat alongside me, quizzed Putin about reports that racism was systemic on Russian football terraces. Putin's bodyguards looked as unhappy as their principal, who dismissed the claims and insisted that racism was not a problem in Russia.

As well as the kickbacks revealed by the US investigation, Putin had played a deviously clever game reflective of the ruthless politician he is. An investigation by the BBC had been transmitted in the days before the Zurich ballot, accusing three voters from FIFA's executive committee of taking kickbacks. In addition, two committee members had been suspended earlier following allegations of wrongdoing made by the *Sunday Times.* Putin had seized on the claims and dismissed them as part of a 'dirty campaign' against FIFA delegates, who were being dragged into the dirt and discredited, he said. He declared the intrepid and genuine efforts by Britain's journalists to investigate FIFA as slanted against the Russian bid and 'unfair competition'.

As he sat on the stage smiling the assassin's smile, it was evident that this was a man who always found a way to get what he wanted. To this day, nothing has changed. And on that night, every honest football lover around the world was unfairly deceived.

England, Not
My England

I WANTED England to be awarded that 2018 World Cup, for a host of reasons. It would have lifted the country, my country, and given me and my fellow journalists years of good copy. I confess, though, that I find it hard to support the football team that represents the land of my birth. The poisonous 'monkey chants' aimed at black players by hateful white spectators on TV's *Match of the Day* and *The Big Match* back when I was a kid still ring in my ears. Looking back, I wonder why Saint and Greavsie did not call them out. Yes, that was a wonderful goal by Millwall's Derek Possee, but Brian Moore – gentleman that you were – I can't remember you using your position of power to highlight to your viewers the racial abuse being meted out. If I could hear it through my TV, then I was damn sure the commentators from their seats and presenters in the studio could hear it too and it pained me that it was all brushed under the carpet.

After the horrific hissing from West Ham supporters to Jewish fans of Tottenham that I had witnessed as a boy, the venom against Asians would also come to enrage me. At an Everton match I once heard opposition fans singing 'I'd rather be a Paki than a Scouse'. As it happened, they were Newport County fans but many others were guilty of it at that time. No wonder the reluctance of Asians to send their sons to football training.

I would also go on to meet football's so-called 'Three Degrees', Laurie Cunningham, Cyrille Regis and Brendon Batson. The latter was also an alumnus of McEntee Senior High in Walthamstow. I once bumped into him on a quiet Sunday morning at a newsagents in Walsall when I was staying at Meera's parents and became starstruck and duly fawned around him. Laurie, who in 1979 became the first British player to sign for Real Madrid and who tragically died in a car accident in Spain aged just 33, was a hero of mine who I saw regularly burning up the touchline for Orient in my youth. My football geekery and research also led me to believe I had an affinity with Cyrille Regis as we shared a birthday, 9 February. I was proud of them as men of colour for living my dream and I understood the higher hurdles they had jumped to make it.

Yet I believed that the labelling of them as 'The Three Degrees' – because they were black and a trio – was born of racism, no matter people saying it was affectionate or that these were different times. Some people might even call it harmless, casual racism and that 'people like me' might be making too much of it, but I don't believe any racism is harmless or casual. People need to be educated about that, and to educate themselves.

The nickname came from a Philadelphia pop group whose heartbreak song 'When Will I See You Again' was said to have been a favourite of King Charles in 1974 when his future queen, Camilla, had married her first husband a year earlier. It was Ron Atkinson who, as manager of West Bromwich Albion, fielded the trio in the late 1970s at a time when racism was rife in stadia and went largely unchallenged. Fair play to him for that. But to my mind, any good work Atkinson did was undermined when he infamously used the N-word referring to the Chelsea defender Marcel Desailly when working as a pundit on ITV. Atkinson thought he was off air but the microphones were still on and picked him up saying, 'He is what is known in some schools as a fucking thick, lazy n***er.' Naturally, it soon got out and Atkinson admitted that his crass comment, broadcast across Dubai and the Middle East, was 'idiotic, stupid and offensive'. The damage was done, however, and Atkinson resigned before he was sacked.

Even before that moment, I already felt uneasy over the branding of his Three Degrees and saw it as laden with racial connotations. Why did these fine footballers, with their individual skills and prowess, deserve to be given a showbusiness title based on their colour? Their strength was their professionalism and dignity. I never heard Atkinson refer to, say, Bryan Robson, Derek Statham, John Wile and Alistair Brown as Slade.

Atkinson grouping his three black professionals together also had undertones for me of some sort of assumption that they should have been grateful as black men for being given a special opportunity. Atkinson wrote in his autobiography: 'If you look at my track record as a manager, I was one of the first managers in the game to give black players a chance.' More than a decade before, however, Ron Greenwood and John Lyall had beaten him to it at West Ham. The point I felt Atkinson had missed was that, by claiming credit for 'giving black players a chance', he had acted as if these players were somehow lucky to get where merit had taken them. It would have been enough to employ the trio and let their football do the talking. Too much talking and not enough thinking it through also led Atkinson into the N-word disgrace. The whole episode illustrated to me how racism and unfounded stereotypical attitudes may have been overtly banished from the airwaves but were still lodged in the minds of some football people.

The modern history of the England team has also been littered with racism in both word and deed perpetrated by some undesirable elements who attach themselves to the cause and bring in dangerous nationalism and a spurious sense of moral and social superiority to justify their beliefs. It can spill into violence and hooliganism, as I saw at the 1998 World Cup in France, my first. That night when England played Tunisia at Marseille's Stade Vélodrome still makes me shudder.

There was no escaping the mayhem which broke out at a fan site and worsened at the Old Port area. Tear gas from the riot police filled the air as bottles and glasses flew in every direction. One England fan taking on around five men turned towards me with blood dripping on to his white national team shirt from a neck wound after being slashed with a knife before he collapsed. The brutality of the evening left me wondering who my enemy was; the North Africans supporting Tunisia or my fellow Englishmen who would probably take one look at my skin and see me as an opposition supporter. The fighting went on for hours and at one stage gangs of England hooligans took over a bar at the corner of the port and began hurling tables and chairs. They were sent running by a mere handful of local lads who rolled their sleeves up, walked calmly to the bar and gave them a good bashing.

All this I observed from the hotel balcony of a veteran football writer who emerged from a taxi after dinner and inquired if anything had been happening but graciously invited the news pack to watch in safety from his room. The battle went on for several hours before police gained control. The long walk back to my Marseille accommodation in the early hours filled me with dread for fear of being attacked either by a Tunisian fan for being English or an English hooligan for looking Tunisian.

That fear and those racists among England fans are why I regularly want England to lose. The best example of this came on 10 December 2022, when I was at the Al Bayt Stadium in Qatar to see England play France in the quarter-finals of the World Cup...

There were close to 69,000 spectators in the ground and I could see that the English supporters were in the majority. It was no surprise to me at all having seen every one of England's World Cup finals' matches since 1998 and witnessed our supporters' passion. I watched as Harry Kane, the England captain, placed the ball on the spot to take the second penalty his team had been awarded after

Théo Hernandez had pushed Mason Mount. Kane had already successfully dispatched a previous penalty award against France's goalkeeper and his Tottenham team-mate Hugo Lloris. Now France were leading 2-1 with just ten minutes left. I was acutely aware that back home there were some 22 million English people watching on TV and praying or begging for him to be successful while others were maybe hiding their eyes.

Professionally it may have been good for sales of papers and hits online if Kane were to score and extend England's chances of reaching the semi-finals, but personally I was probably the only Englishman in the stadium who was indifferent. In fact, being entirely truthful, I longed for Lloris to dive full stretch and palm the ball to safety or for Kane to fall on his backside as he kicked the ball, just as John Terry did in the 2008 Champions League Final in Moscow against Manchester United when his fall led to him hitting the woodwork and Chelsea losing the final.

Kane stepped up as English hearts beat faster and nails were chewed, his gentlemanly manager Gareth Southgate watching on from the sidelines.

Whenever England take a penalty or head for a shoot-out, memories always surface of witnessing Southgate's miss at Wembley in the 1996 Euros semi-final against Germany but Kane so rarely misses; surely there would be an English eruption of joy. Kane stared at the ball, took four quick steps and lashed it over the bar. There was despondency on the English faces around me. Me? I was just relieved. I even joked to a colleague that Kane's spot kick was probably over Lausanne now and that FIFA would never get that ball back.

I have been in this situation with England many times before. When David Beckham kicked out foolishly at the Argentine Diego Simeone in the round-of-16 match in 1998 in Saint-Étienne, I was close enough to see the Argentine's theatrics and mock pain. Beckham walked off below me, with manager Glenn Hoddle ignoring him, and he became public enemy number one. His red card was followed by England losing on penalties in a game where the Argentinians had been on the back foot for much of the match. I thought Beckham had done me a favour, and I pitied my fellow east London lad for the hate and loathing that came his way. There was even an effigy of him hung in public. Similarly, when Croatia's Mario Mandžukić scored late in extra time at Moscow's Luzhniki Stadium to knock England out in the 2018 semi-finals, my overwhelming emotion was not sadness at England missing the chance to play in a World Cup Final for the first time in 52 years.

I have tried to explain it to my England-loving and football-mad nephews – whose passions are exercised on Hull City, Newcastle, West Ham and England – that I don't hate my country. Southgate's is the most representative England squad we have seen in terms of background and diversity, but my reasons for preferring defeat for the national team are solely due to the xenophobic history surrounding the team and the thuggery and racism I have witnessed while reporting their games.

In fact, I love my country of birth and, having travelled the seven seas and lived in the United States for two and a half years, I can safely say I was born in the best country in the world, even though it has a shameful past with the Raj occupying my motherland for almost a century and then suppressing it from my school history lessons. In the classroom, I was taught all about the Industrial Revolution, Tarmacadam, and other events like the demise of Harold II at the Battle of Hastings in 1066. But it was my family educating me and my own research as a young man that led me to the hidden truth about Britain's imperialism and the vile British East India Company. I have seen the bullet holes that remain to this day in the walls of Jallianwala Bagh in Amritsar where Brigadier-General Reginald Dyer ordered the massacre of up to 1,500 Indian innocents by gunfire, but during my entire school life the despicable Raj and this type of outrage were never mentioned in a classroom. Lord Mountbatten's 'At the stroke of the midnight hour' nonsense speech, when India was divided and given its independence, created sectarian violence, religious cleansing and a huge refugee crisis that crushed my family too. Many of them took the horrors they endured or witnessed silently to the grave.

Therefore, whenever I hear England football fans singing 'Ten German bombers' at World Cups or insulting Scottish fans by labelling them as 'sweaties', or when I come across any of these foul-mouthed louts on foreign shores racially abusing others, in my subconscious they are hateful people cut from the same cloth as Dyer, the murdering butcher of Amritsar. I hear 'Ten German Bombers' and the sound of the bullets being fired at the innocents of Amritsar echo. The colonialism Dyer and his invading comrades enforced on India has tainted any affection I might have grown to feel for the Three Lions. Maybe an apology for the death and destruction caused would have helped – and it still might. Greece and Britain have a long-standing dispute over the Elgin Marbles, known less possessively these days as the Parthenon Sculptures. Perhaps Britain could return the Koh-i-Noor diamond to India? It is time Britain started facing up to the mayhem caused around the world and acknowledged it by teaching children in the classroom. The glorious bravery of our troops during the World Wars are crucially important to our past; but so are the cowardly days of the Raj.

The past has shaped my feelings about England winning a major trophy and the licence I believe that would give for the insufferable swagger of the xenophobes and racists whose noise and chanting often overwhelm the genuine fans forced to endure 'The Great Escape' tune ringing in their ears on the terraces. (Why play a tune from a war film at a football match?) I've thought long and hard, searched my soul, about why I cannot support England at football. It's not the same when England play Australia for the Ashes or when our wonderful athletes competed at the seven Olympic Games I have reported from. It is only football where my patriotism has been poisoned. I do support India at cricket, though, and would thus fail that ridiculous Norman Tebbit test, when the Tory politician insisted that a test of Englishness was supporting the England cricket team. What, even when I was born here? And what of those who emigrated from these shores to Australia? I'm sure English people living in this country have no problem with exiles continuing to feel English during an Ashes series.

Sir Andy Murray was berated for an anti-English joke he made as a youngster. It was accepted as a crass attempt at simply being humorous, but the Wimbledon champion is aware of the football animosity shown towards Scotland and its fans – which in fairness is often reciprocated. Personally,

I can't joke about the stuff I have seen and heard. I always found it galling when our national anthem was turned into a political attack on Irish Republicans at England matches. Indeed, the bloodshed and slaying of innocents by both the IRA and nationalists during the Troubles was sickening and tragic, but football fans singing 'No surrender' and 'scum' has only fuelled fires that should have been doused long ago.

My resentment is further stoked by the silence that often surrounds Britain's colonial past – unless such achievements as transport links and cricket are being highlighted by the Masters of the Raj. Thankfully, historians such as Sathnam Sanghera, the journalist who wrote the excellent book *Empireland* and followed it up with *Empireworld*, have chronicled it all for future generations.

The question of my support is not simple, but nuanced, as I have seen the joy that the national team brings when it progresses at tournaments. A wonder strike from Harry Kane or a thundering headed goal by Harry Maguire always lifts the nation's mood, and I would not deny my decent fellow countrymen and women those moments of joy and hope. Before my attitude towards England set in – indeed, before as a kid I grew interested in the history of my heritage – I was also a passionate supporter. I was seven years old when Bobby Moore lifted the World Cup for England but too young to remember much or share in the fervour and celebrations that gripped England for years. Four years later, though, when England went to Mexico in 1970 to defend the trophy, I was an ardent England fan. I watched with awe on my parents' black and white television as Bobby Charlton and Geoff Hurst played a group game against the Brazil of Pelé. Everyone talked about the magic of the Brazilians but, for me, the wizards from England were greater. I could not stop myself jumping around whenever Moore led his team out. Not even the scandal surrounding him being accused of stealing a bracelet before the tournament could taint my love; it just couldn't be true. He had been detained in Bogota, Colombia on a stopover while England were flying back to Mexico from two friendlies. The bracelet had apparently disappeared from a hotel shop and the story dominated the television news and papers for days before Moore was cleared and freed.

I watched the Brazil game on the family TV as my father and his friends smoked Woodbines and played rummy with their hard-earned cash, my father occasionally roaring when picking up his winnings. I recall my Uncle Chishtie roaring with laughter when he shouted at the TV: 'Agaya, Yea Bobby Chore!' (He is here, Bobby the thief.) In Punjabi the word *chore* means thief and the rhyme with Bobby's surname had the room in stitches. I fled the room in tears at what I saw as disrespect, returning only to see both Francis Lee and Jeff Astle go close, before Jairzinho scored with a sweet shot that won the game for the Brazilians.

Fortunately, England won their other two games in the group, by 1-0 scorelines against Czechoslovakia and Romania. I can see it as clearly as if it were yesterday: Hurst picked up a pass from Lee and smashed the ball home with his left foot against Romania. The excitement overtook me as I tried to copy his amazing effort, much to the bemusement of my family. As I swung my foot in a copycat strike – well, in my imagination – my black Tuf slip-on shoe became loose and flew through the air, shattering a small panel in the kitchen window. When my idols went out of the tournament in the quarter-finals, England having lost 3-2 to West Germany after being 2-0 up, for days I could hardly speak about football or listen to their tournament anthem 'Back Home', which until then had been on repeat.

Over the next six years or so, through my teenage years, my support waned the more I read the history that I wasn't being taught at school, and the more I saw and heard all that racism on the terraces.

These days the thugs have social media to amplify their shouting, often hiding behind the anonymity it offers. My feeling that their racism has never gone away, but just been largely controlled and quietened by Gareth Southgate's enlightenment, was confirmed when Marcus Rashford, Jadon Sancho and Bukayo Saka were targeted with racist abuse after missing penalties against Italy in the Euro 2020 Final. Here I was, some 40-plus years on after the monkey chanting and racial violence and abuse first came to my attention, and it was clear – no matter any progress that might have been made – that there remained a long road ahead.

Heavier punishment is needed. It is time players walked off the pitch – both sets – at the first sound of any monkey chanting or abuse. Clubs need to weed out racists and take responsibility for their fans. Season-ticket holders should be given reminders that we all lose out to racism. Points deductions like those meted out to clubs who fall foul of financial fair play regulations are long overdue. Yes, it would hit the fans and the blameless players, and there might be protests at three lost points that could cost a club a title, promotion or even mean relegation, but it would be the best way to ram home the message that racist chanting has been going on too long and it has to stop.

It cannot be denied that the Football Association has worked hard to combat racism, and Southgate's sincere words always resonate, as do the gestures of his captain Harry Kane and his team-mates when they take the knee as part of the Black Lives Matter campaign. Things are better, it is true. But having seen so much to disturb me as a journalist and man of Asian heritage, it seems unlikely I will be recapturing the innocence and joy of my England-supporting childhood any time soon.

Prague Spring

WEST HAM trophies have been few and far between in my lifetime. I was too young to remember the 1964 FA Cup triumph and the European Cup-Winners' Cup win the following year. As for the 1975 and 1980 FA Cups, it was a case of looking on at a distance, thrilled but not right in the action as I so desired to be.

In 1975, at 16 I was too young and unworldly to know how to secure a ticket for the final against Fulham. How I wish I'd been there... my hero Bobby Moore making his last ever appearance at Wembley – now as a Fulham player in the twilight of his career. I watched again on my parents' black and white TV as two goals by Alan Taylor from inside the six-yard area in the last 30 minutes secured the

Cup. I felt for Bobby, but leapt over the sofa at the final whistle, screaming. The next day I ventured out to East Ham to see the Newham Town Hall tribute and parade and to this day I beam whenever I recall Frank Lampard Snr waving and smiling directly at me from a window of the building as his team-mates showed off the trophy.

Five years on, not much had changed when it came to getting hold of a Wembley ticket, thanks to financial issues and a lack of connections. The only difference was that this time my parents now owned a 21-inch colour National Panasonic TV and I watched West Ham, who had then dropped into the Second Division, beat First Division Arsenal 1-0 with a rare Trevor Brooking header. The gold of the Arsenal shirts glistened from the colour TV, but there was nothing bright about the tackle Willie Young inflicted on 17-year-old Paul Allen, who had been put through by Brooking and only had Pat Jennings to beat when Young scythed him down. It was a disgraceful foul that would have earned a red card and a three-match ban today. My mother had made me my favourite chapati and rajma red bean dish and the food nearly flew up from the table and across the room as I raged over the deliberate foul. Allen must to this day rue the moment Young robbed him of teenage Wembley glory and a place in FA Cup history.

Sir Trevor has often been asked since about whether he meant to head the ball in as he was falling over or whether he was trying to evade a wild shot from Stuart Pearson that was flying across the six-yard box. In 2020, the team held a celebration in Essex to commemorate the 40th anniversary of the great day, and among those who showed up were Sir Trevor, Billy Bonds, Alan Devonshire and Ray Stewart. I was also in the audience and delighted to hear Sir Trevor definitively end all controversy by stating that it was a deliberate header and not a lucky deflection that saw off the showboating Gunners. At the London Stadium in recent years, I have also chatted to Alan Taylor as a fan and thanked him for his 1975 FA Cup double but, though these are enjoyable moments, they are secondary experiences. I had always been waiting for a glorious, historic and personal West Ham moment that one day I would be able to tell my grandchildren about and say that I was there. Now, at last, the time had come.

It was Wednesday, 7 June 2023. The venue was the 19,370-seater Eden Arena in Prague and it was just before 11pm. Jarrod Bowen was clear of the last Fiorentina defender and racing towards the opposing goal, having been fed a slick pass from the Brazilian Lucas Paquetá. Out of the corner of my eye, I could see thousands of West Ham fans rising to their feet, heads stretched like meerkats, to see if he could do it. Could Bowen place the ball into the net in the very last minute and bring West Ham United the Europa Conference League trophy, the club's first real silverware in 43 years?

He could. Bowen slotted the ball past the forlorn goalkeeper and in a blink, he was running towards the corner flag and sliding on his knees in front of thousands of screaming West Ham supporters as his team-mates rushed to hug and congratulate him. Meanwhile, manager David Moyes was storming down the touchline, fists clenched in triumph. This was the club's long-awaited moment of glory and their fans in the ground went wild.

My heart was beating faster and faster, yet I sat perfectly still and unmoved up in the press box as my fingers began tapping on my laptop keyboard.

I had traded my love and passion for West Ham for professional impartiality and so I was following the press box's unwritten rule of not showing emotion towards either team, no matter the result. Before long, the Spanish referee Carlos del Cerro Grande blew the final whistle. The Hammers had secured a 2-1 victory and the trophy. On the outside I appeared cool, keeping my eyes focused on my keyboard. Inside, I was bursting with emotion but holding back tears as I was seated alongside some of Britain's best sportswriters, who revel in taking themselves seriously (as I know this from years of invading their turf as a news reporter and seeing the self-importance of many of them). And so it was in silence that my heart filled with pride and joy that night as I watched Declan Rice collect the trophy, run towards the West Ham fans and drop to his knees to share the moment.

It was the same later as I listened to Moyes and Bowen at their press conference. Bowen had placed his Man of the Match award, a miniature replica of the Conference League trophy, on the table and it glistened. This had been the most glorious moment in more than 50 years as a West Ham fan but somehow it was also one of the loneliest. Both Moyes and Bowen looked as if they didn't want to be there. I got it. This was the biggest moment of their careers and downstairs in the dressing room the drink would be flowing and the dancing in full swing. I wanted to climb over the rows of reporters and on to that stage and thank them, hug them tightly and sing 'I'm Forever Blowing Bubbles' while waving my West Ham scarf that I had concealed in my laptop bag.

I was in a complete daze for some hours after the final whistle. It really was a case of 'what just happened?' as I made my way back to the centre of Prague, having filed thousands of words back to London. For so long, I had been a West Ham sufferer. A footballing life filled with painful disappointment. There was the FA Cup semi-final against Nottingham Forest, the League Cup semi-final with Stoke City, the Littlewoods Cup semi-final defeat by Luton Town, the 2004 play-off final loss to Crystal Palace. And of course that bitter defeat in the FA Cup Final of 2006 against Liverpool through the wonderful last-minute equaliser by Steven Gerrard to be followed by the heartbreaking penalty shoot-out. So many other desperate nights of travelling home from all over England, sometimes in foul weather, after yet another embarrassing defeat to teams from lower divisions. All these were forgotten on this night. I thought of the team's homecoming in an open-top bus through the East End with adoring fans looking on proudly. It was a parade I knew I would miss due to having to stay on an extra day in case there were any major dramas like fan arrests or violence. There had, after all, been a few skirmishes before the match.

At 2am, my photographer colleague Peter Powell and I managed to find a corner shop able to provide us with eight large cans of warm Czech beer. We proceeded to our hotel lobby and cracked open a few cans while I bored my Liverpool-supporting snapper with my observations about how West Ham would be taken more seriously by Premier League clubs and supporters now that we had conquered Europe. It was almost as if decades of pain were leaving my body and my mind.

The reality was the hotel night porter looking at us bored, his body language and watch-checking indicating that he felt the West Ham party was over and that it was time to retire to our rooms. In fact, the party was just starting. If there is a football god, he or she was looking down on me at that very moment. I had spent the days in Prague preceding the final unsuccessfully trying to locate the West Ham hotel. This was, in equal measure, for both professional and fanboy reasons. Now, from nowhere, my prayers had been answered as the team bus pulled up outside our hotel.

I dashed outside but was quickly disappointed: what with the tinted windows and the darkness of the night, the coach looked empty. My heart sank. Then, all of a sudden, the middle door of the coach swung open and my heroes emerged. First was David Moyes, then Mark Noble – two men who had given so much to the West Ham faithful. It was fitting that Noble should be right at the centre of the celebrations having devoted his whole career so manfully to the club.

Just a few West Ham fans were around, but between us we formed a guard of honour for the players as they descended from the bus. On the other side of the line, I could see the photographer's flash gun emitting light every time he pressed his camera shutter, holding his camera with one hand. On his other wrist was the white plastic bag containing the beers we still had left, which almost had him lopsided because of the weight of the cans.

When Alphonse Areola, the goalkeeper who had played such a big part in the triumph, emerged down the coach steps, he was carrying a portable music box. He pressed a button and that catchy pop song 'Freed From Desire' by Gala Rizzatto, which is said to be an anthem of empowerment and liberation, boomed out. Not that West Ham fans see it that way. Their rendition has the line 'Bowen's on fire and he's shagging Dani Dyer', of his relationship with the daughter of *EastEnders* star Danny Dyer. Anyway, it was the signal for the dancing to begin. There was Pablo Fornals spinning round and round, then reserve goalkeeper Łukasz Fabiański – who had initially put his fingers to his lips to silence the West Ham faithful and avoid waking hotel guests – joined in. He was followed by Thilo Kehrer, Saïd Benrahma, Maxwell Cornet and Ben Johnson, who hugged a fan next to me. I wanted to hug Ben too. Danny Ings, Aaron Cresswell, Manuel Lanzini,

Nayef Aguerd and Gianluca Scamacca, whose goals in the earlier rounds had helped get West Ham to Prague, all emerged smiling too.

By now I was singing along and had to keep myself from not jumping into the dancing with our heroes. Captain Declan Rice surfaced to high-five my fellow fans, waving his hands to encourage the dancing, and was followed by Bowen. I shouted my congratulations. Paquetá stopped to sign a fan's shirt before being bundled away by West Ham's security detail, his arm raised in the air to acknowledge the adoring supporters. It lasted barely 90 seconds, but it helped release some of the emotion that I had concealed in the name of professionalism.

The next day, I drank a beer or three in Prague's historic Old Town Square – while our Hammers were back in the East End parading the trophy from an open-top bus – and was overjoyed to find that several thousand West Ham supporters were still in town. There was no need to run from them now, 50 years on, thankfully. I recalled a day when I watched a West Ham match on a TV in a pub in New York, where I was working at the time, with Bill Gardner, one of West Ham's most infamous football hooligans and who wrote a book about the notorious Inter City Firm on which the film *Green Street* was based. He was always against the vile 'Paki-bashing' meted out in the seventies, he said, but apologetically told me: 'Them were different times. But I'd never go after any West Ham fan.' We became friends and have kept in touch.

Now, there are football supporters, particularly followers of London rivals Tottenham, Arsenal and Chelsea, who do their best to decry West Ham's European triumph. To the Spurs fans, who include my elder brother Bipin Kumar, I point out that they were not in Europe the following year. The Gooners and the Stamford Bridge lot are equally full of disdain at our triumph and probably think they have bragging rights, having reached the Champions League Final (Arsenal) or won the trophy (Chelsea). But they would not now be able to sing, as I did with my fellow Billy Bonds Stand season-ticket holders at the London Stadium: 'We know who we are. . . Champions of Europe, we know who we are.' There was an enjoyable, unique moment in the early stages of the 23/24 season when Manchester City fans and ourselves sang it together at the London Stadium when the two clubs met in a Premier League match.

To us it was not some 'Mickey Mouse' trophy or some European third tier success, as some of the elite believed. It prompted a spring in our step now and a belief that West Ham belonged in the upper echelons of the Premier League, capable of turning over the big clubs. For the elite, more moneyed clubs, I sometimes feel that success can spoil their fans and a sense of entitlement can grow. West Ham supporters have accepted that there will be low points, possibly including relegations that are just not going to happen to such as the big Manchester clubs or others in London, and we have come to recognise the highs of rare trophies as precious bonuses to a life of footballing uncertainty that makes our club both maddening and loveable. We know who we are...

One other thing about that Prague trip brings me pleasure and even consolation. In the days before the final Meera was herself flying to Prague to shoot a drama called *Wheel of Time* for Amazon Prime TV and she filmed a planeful of West Ham supporters singing 'Bubbles' on her phone and posted it to her 44,000 followers on X, formerly Twitter. 'Well,' she said in the caption, 'I had an unexpectedly jolly flight to Prague this evening.' She's never going to become a Hammers fan, or indeed a football follower, but at least she had finally experienced a genuine, warm and innocent fan moment surrounding the game to help replace her previous experience of racism and give her a memory that this time would make her smile. And that made me smile too.

Acknowledgements

THANKS TO the inspirational Ian Ridley for asking me to write this book and then skilfully, diplomatically and gently guiding me from the beginning to this very page.

I am also grateful to family, friends and colleagues who have journeyed with me or encouraged me along the way by pitching in…

There have been many people who have showed kindness, patience, professional and loving support and, indeed, mentored me.

For those reasons my gratitude goes to:

Ian Walker, Hugh Dougherty, Charles Garside, Dorothy Byrne, Steve Anderson, Anton Antonowicz, Jeremy Armstrong, Rajeev Syal, Nihal Arthanayake, Jeremy Selwyn, Rodney

Hinds, Ian Gallagher, Mihir Bose, Robert Jobson, Kim Sengupta, Suri Krishnamma, Henry Bonsu, Nick Edwards, Ruben Riggins, Hugh Muir, Pedro Carvalho, Abul Taher, Nick Parker, Amar Singh, Amit Roy, Iqbal Wahhab, Danny Groom, David Instone, Martin Brunt, Jenny McCartney, Keith Richmond, David Luddy, Keith Dovkants, Keith Stretten, Kulvinder Ghir, Nicole Wilmshurst, John Sturgis, Louise Flood, Yasmin Whitaker-Khan, Pat Wykes,Maryam Ishaq, Anthony France, Ashish Joshi, Yasmeen Khan, Dave Benett, Anita Anand, Jerry Lawton, Holly Kitchen, Rohan Suri. Nathaniel Jones, Gordon Warnecke, Luke Bhatia, Kiran Rai, Inderdeep Bains, John Wragg, Jim Murray, Nick Craven, KP Sailesh, Lawrence Lustig, Jeff Moore, Cyril Dixon, Annie Leask, John Twomey, Geoff Pugh, Peter Allen,Nikhil Rai, Norman Y Lono, Vivek Singh, Phil O'Brien, Gurukh Johal, Dave O'Field, Puja Vedi, Russell Myers, Suki Dusanj-Lenz, Gustavo Valiente, Jim Gallagher, Peter Powell, Paul Thompson, Amy Iggulden, Andy Gardner, John Cross, Raith al-Samarrai, Eddie Mulholland, Jack Lefley, Steve Double, Colin Grainger, Sami Mokbel, Vikram Dodd, Harcharan Chandhoke,

ACKNOWLEDGEMENTS

Jackie Murray, Darren Lewis, Vai Bhardwaj, Laura Collins, Jae Donnelly, Rob Singh, Lucy Cockcroft, Sarah Festa, Humphrey Nemar, Yasmin Alibhai-Brown, Max Kitchen, Shyama Perera, Alan McKinlay, Annette Witheridge and Meera Syal.

**London,
March 2024**

The author has donated part of his fee for writing this book to the Bobby Moore Cancer Fund.

FOOTBALL SHORTS

2023 marked the successful launch of the series, with three great books …

Pantomime Hero

Jimmy Armfield

*Memories of the man who
lifted Leeds after Brian Clough*

By Ian Ridley

The Homecoming

The Lionesses and Beyond

By Jane Purdon

Blue was the Colour

A Tale of Tarnished Love

By Andy Hamilton

All available individually for £9.99 each, signed by the authors, or £25 for the set of three at www.football-shorts.co.uk.

And 2024 brings another terrific trio of superb short reads …

Double Acts

A Modern History of Tottenham in
10½ Strike Partnerships

By Julie Welch

Following *Namaste, Geezer* November will mark the release of the brilliant David Winner's perceptive and incisive analysis of Gareth Southgate's tenure as England manager, how he changed the mood of the national team, and how it all panned out at Euro '24. David, the author of such classics as *Brilliant Orange* and *Those Feet*, will place the Southgate reign in the context of the nation's social and political landscape.

Each of this year's books – signed by the author – can be ordered from Football Shorts at £9.99 or £25 for the set of three. Just go to www.football-shorts.co.uk or scan the QR code below.